GW00322352

YouTube
WORLD
RECORDS

DON'T TRY THIS AT HOME

Some of this book's clips feature stunts performed either by professionals or under the supervision of professionals. Accordingly the publishers must insist that no one attempt to re-create or re-enact any stunt or activity performed on the featured videos.

THIS IS A CARLTON BOOK

Published by Carlton Books Ltd
20 Mortimer Street
London W1T 3JW

Text and design © 2018 Carlton Books Ltd

All rights reserved. No part of this publication may be reproduced, stored in a retrieval system, or transmitted in any form or by any means (including electronic, mechanical, photocopying, recording, or otherwise) without prior written permission from the publisher.

ISBN 978-1-78739-161-1

Project Editor: Chris Mitchell
Design: Katie Baxendale, Andri Johannsson
Production: Lisa Hedicker
Picture Research: Steve Behan, Paul Langan

A CIP catalogue for this book is available from the British Library

Printed in Dubai

10 9 8 7 6 5 4 3 2

YouTube

WORLD
RECORDS

ADRIAN BESLEY

CARLTON
BOOKS

CONTENTS

INTRODUCTION

Welcome to the only records book that enables you to see the records being broken for yourself. Enter the short URL or scan the QR code into your phone, tablet, laptop or computer and witness history being made across the world.

The fastest, biggest, highest, thinnest – all over the world people are united by a fascination with human achievements. We all love a record breaker. Whether it is a hundredth of a second being shaved off a famous sporting record or the first recording of a fantastically bizarre new category, we share a fascination with discovering who and what. Till now, the only thing missing has been our chance to actually see the record-breakers in action ...

That's where YouTube comes in. This global resource is open to anyone to upload their videos. It contains literally thousands of record-breaking clips, from the most well-known to the completely obscure. Some have millions of views, while others remain virtually undiscovered.

Among the gems available to view are Usain Bolt's amazing 100-metre sprint; the longest time spent by a human in virtual reality; the fastest speed reached by a human in an Ironman-esque jet suit; the man who spent over an hour with a beard of bees on his face; a woman with the world's strongest hair; and the bunny who can slam dunk with the best of them!

This book is your guide to the best of the record-breaking videos on YouTube. It leads you to the most exciting, the most thrilling, the most interesting and the most ridiculous videos on the site. Just read through the brief description and then use the short URL address or the QR code to access the clip – all, of course, completely for free.

HIGH-FLYING RECORDS

Don't look down! It's time to meet some of the sky-high heroes of the record-breaking world. These are some vertigo-immune daredevils who don't know the meaning of fear.

The Wing King

http://y2u.be/eHPZPNzJwLA

On a hot day in May 2017, Fraser Corsan jumped from a plane, 35,508 feet (10,823 metres) above the Californian desert. It's minus 137 degrees Celsius and all he's wearing is a wingsuit, but Fraser is a man on a mission. He was aiming to break a handful of records, but atmospheric conditions have limited him to one: pure speed. On exiting the plane, Fraser immediately hit a speed of 249 mph. He was going so fast that he saw cars going backwards on a motorway, five miles (8 kilometres) directly below him – fast enough to make him the world's fastest unassisted human.

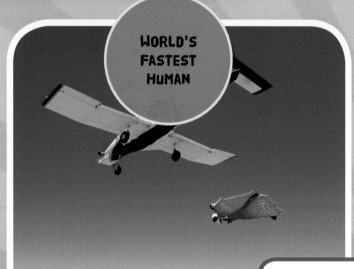

WORLD'S FASTEST HUMAN

MOST ROPE JUMPERS TOGETHER

◀ 1,2,3… Jump

http://y2u.be/6SvExJadB78

When your mum says, "And if all your friends jumped off a bridge, would you do it too?" show her this clip. There are 245 of them, many of them probably friends, on a bridge in Hortolandia, near Sao Paulo, Brazil. On the signal, they all jump together from the 98-foot (30-metre) high bridge. Oh, and they're bound together and suspended from the bridge with rope. These thrill-seekers are not bungee jumpers but rope jumpers – their supporting lines having no elasticity – and never before have so many leapt into the unknown en masse.

Takes the Biscuit

http://y2u.be/UBf7WC19lpw

The lengths the Brits will go to for the love of tea and biscuits, eh? In 2016, Simon Berry from Yorkshire, England, took a 240-foot (73-metre) bungee dive to dunk his biscuit into his cup of tea. Clasping both wrists together like a diver to achieve the necessary precision, Simon's jump was perfectly judged to allow his extended hand to dip his chocolate Hobnob halfway into his freshly brewed cuppa. And, to complete a perfect plunge, the biscuit was still intact and nicely half melted when he returned to the platform. It was the highest bungee dunk ever.

▶

Over the Edge

http://y2u.be/-9ox62y4zsE

Imagine taking a leap from, say, the top of the Leaning Tower of Pisa, past jagged rocks and into a small pool beneath. In August 2015, in a world-record cliff-jump attempt, Brazilian-born daredevil Laso Schaller plunged almost 200 feet (60 metres) from a ledge into Switzerland's famed Cascata del Salto waterfall. Six oxygen tents were aerating the water in order to give him a softer landing, but Schaller hit the water outside of his intended landing zone – at a speed of around 76 mph (123 km/h). This high-quality video shows the death-defying jump from every angle, including the view from a camera mounted to his helmet.

HIGHS AND LOWS

These record-breakers have gone to extreme heights (or as low as they can go) in order to get their names in the record-books.

▼ Skate Limbo

http://y2u.be/7HEPRZuRWvc

Like many young kids, Gagan Satish, a Bangalore schoolboy, loves to get out on his rollerskates. Not many have a talent like Gagan's though. He skated nearly 230 feet (70 metres) with his face just 5 inches (12.7 centimetres) from the ground – passing under 39 cars on the way! Gagan has only been rollerskating for three years, but, even more incredibly, he is only six years old. Obviously, his experience helped him break the record; the previous holder was only five!

CHAMPION LIMBO ROLLER SKATER

Breathtaking!

http://y2u.be/YtryV9qItsg

Next time you're at your local swimming pool, see how long you can hold your breath underwater. Can you do 30 seconds? Or maybe 45, if you really fill your lungs? This exercise will give you some appreciation of Canadian William Winram's 2013 record dive into the Dead Sea at Sharm el-Sheikh in Egypt. Will took a single breath and held it for 3 minutes and 8 seconds, using a sled to help him descend 475 feet (145 metres) – for comparison, New York's Statue of Liberty is just 300 feet (92 metres) high – and a rope and monofin to speed his return to the surface.

WORLD
RECORD FOR
HIGHEST FREE
SLACKLINING

A Lot of Hot Air

http://y2u.be/wv9P9e7i82E

Ivan Trifonov is a ballooning pioneer. The Austrian aeronaut has held four world records for hot-air ballooning and was the first person to balloon over the South and North Poles. His latest record is even more spectacular as he achieved the first successful balloon journey to the bottom of the 676-foot (206-metre) deep Mamet cave in Obrovac, Croatia. The specially designed balloon saw Trifonov sitting on two gas cylinders, rather than inside a traditional basket, and the descent took 25 minutes. It was the combination of skill and climatic fortune that makes him believe his record will never be broken.

WORLD'S
BEST
BALLOONIST

▲ No Slacking

http://y2u.be/p-6RHjC_SvE

Is tightrope walking a little too safe for you? Try slacklining – walking across flexible, rubber band-type webbing. Still no rush? Then highlining is for you. That's slacklining hundreds, or even thousands, of feet above ground. This beautifully shot video featuring Friedi Kühne's world record longest free solo slackline lasts 38 seconds, but perfectly captures the adrenaline appeal and danger of the sport. 'Free' means walking without a safety harness, but Friedi seems fearless as he walks a 328-foot (110-metre) line over the 656-foot (200-metre) high Verdon Gorge, in the Alpes-de-Haute-Provence in the South of France.

YOUTUBE HITS RECORDS

In just over 10 years, YouTube has grown to be a part of the daily lives of millions of people. No surprise, then, that it now has its own illustrious record-holders.

▶ Puerto Style

http://y2u.be/kJQP7kiw5Fk

"Despacito" – officially the most-watched video on YouTube – has around 4.5 billion views. Yep. That's equivalent to more than every other person in the whole wide world watching it at least once – and some of them don't even have Wi-Fi! The Latin mega-hit by Luis Fonsi, featuring Daddy Yankee, was posted on 12 January 2017 and took the video world by storm. *Despacito* might mean "slowly" in English, but the video, a nothing-special picture of a day in Puerto Rico, sped to the heights of most-watched video on YouTube, surging past Wiz Khalifa's 2015 hit "See You Again" and Psy's former record-setter "Gangnam Style" from 2012.

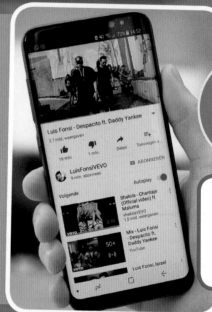

YOUTUBE'S MOST WATCHED VIDEO

◀ A Piece of Cake

http://y2u.be/q53HUAKB9oU

Cookery is the new pop; recipes and foodie videos are a rapidly growing area on YouTube. With a channel that boasts more than 9 million subscribers and an average of 75 million views per month, American baker Rosanna Pansino is one of the most popular creators of foodie content online. Her much-liked Nerdy Nummies series features how-to bakes based on TV shows, books and films, from *Fantastic Beasts* Strudel to *Pirates of the Caribbean* chicken pie. This is the breakout video, though, and Rosanna's Anna and Elsa princess cakes have been devoured in over 170 million views. Yummy!

Reality Check

http://y2u.be/IVaBvyzuypw

The future has arrived – again. Virtual reality is here. For mere pocket money you can buy a cardboard set that enables you to enjoy a simulated physical presence in a virtual or imaginary environment. And it's those innovative popsters, Gorillaz, who've made the biggest splash. Their surreal 360° virtual-reality video for the track "Saturnz Barz" picked up 7 million views in just one month, a YouTube record for the biggest debut of a VR video. However, with music and corporate big hitters about to dip their toes in the VR stream, this is one record that may not last long.

Charlie Still Bites

http://y2u.be/_OBlgSz8sSM

YouTube charts these days are dominated by music videos and children's TV shows, but one great exception refuses to die. In May 2007, a 56-second video of a young boy and his baby brother sitting side by side was posted on YouTube. 'Charlie Bit My Finger – Again!' became a YouTube phenomenon. It was sweet, cheeky and full of infectious laughter, and for years it competed with Miley, Justin and Taylor at the top of the viewing charts. Even now – with around 850 million views – it continues to be the most-watched "home video" on the site – the greatest viral video of them all.

▲ Listen to TED

http://y2u.be/_QdPW8JrYzQ

TED talks have become a YouTube institution. The talks, which tend to last around 10 minutes, span every genre and are entertaining, often fascinating, always expertly delivered and a complete treat for the curious. Some are given by familiar names, such as Stephen Hawking or Bill Gates; others by academics, business leaders and politicians. This is the most popular TED talk ever. It features British stand-up comedian James Veitch giving a laugh-aloud talk entitled, 'This is what happens when you reply to spam email'. So far it has garnered 17 million views – 3 million more than any other TED talk.

MOST WATCHED TED TALK EVER

13

SPEED AND ACCURACY

Another selection of quick-on-the-draw records. Here accuracy is just as important as speed: one false move could mean death, a dodgy haircut or a customer questioning their receipt.

▶ Bully for Them

http://y2u.be/S7zeFMC5J1c

Australian YouTuber outfit How Ridiculous are rather keen on launching things – watermelons, bottle rockets, basketballs, themselves. You get the picture. Here the guys take on the longest ever distance to hit a bullseye on a dartboard. Being cheeky, they get themselves a little help from gravity and drop the darts from a 150-foot (45-metre) tower. That sounds pretty easy, doesn't it? So how many darts do you think it takes them to hit the bull? If you like this, you might want to check out the boys' highest basketball-shot record too.

▶ Join the Club

http://y2u.be/6MGlIE2UlII

Yeah, juggling – I know. It's definitely the most boring of circus skills, but put your prejudice aside and watch this guy in action because it's pretty amazing. In September 2016, before busy rail commuters at Toronto's Union Station, Cirque du Soleil's Rudolf Janecek became the fastest five-club juggler in the world. In a whirl of silver clubs and lightning hands, Rudolph shuffles along as he completes 429 rotations over 30 seconds. In fact, Rudolf threw and caught the clubs so fast that the adjudicators had to review the video in slow-motion before awarding him the record.

FASTEST CLUB JUGGLER

14

◀ Speed Freak

http://y2u.be/dvnmrHS3d9s

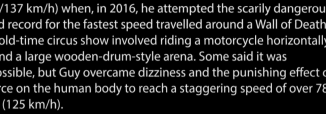

British motorcyclist and TV presenter Guy Martin has a passion for speed and danger. He already held world records for the fastest speed on a gravity-powered snow sled (83 mph/134 km/h) and fastest speed in a soapbox (85 mph/137 km/h) when, in 2016, he attempted the scarily dangerous world record for the fastest speed travelled around a Wall of Death. This old-time circus show involved riding a motorcycle horizontally around a large wooden-drum-style arena. Some said it was impossible, but Guy overcame dizziness and the punishing effect of G-force on the human body to reach a staggering speed of over 78 mph (125 km/h).

▼ Crack the Whip

http://y2u.be/C9FsGHM6AaY

THE FASTEST WHIPPER IN THE WORLD

Indiana Jones eat your heart out. Nathan 'Whippy' Griggs is the whip king of the world and has the records to prove it. He holds the fastest records with both one and two hands, and possesses the longest whip in the world at over 329 feet 7.5 inches (100 metres) long (you can see that on YouTube too – check the sidebar). Wielding 6-foot 7-inch (2-metre) whips made of kangaroo leather, Nathan demonstrates stamina, skill and incredible co-ordination as he amasses 614 cracks in a minute using two whips. And, in case you're interested, that crack you hear is the whip breaking the sound barrier – over 750 mph (1,200 km/h).

A Brush with Fame

http://y2u.be/eXPJo1f60j0

Like most children, Dipanshu Mishra was probably told to clean his teeth at least twice a day. Now I'm sure Dipanshu always polishes up his pearly whites diligently, but he's also been practising with the brush to earn his place among the record breakers. His is a strange record, but one that is oddly compelling to watch, for Dipanshu balances a spinning basketball on the end of his toothbrush – and he keeps it spinning for an astonishing 42.92 seconds. That's quite a feat, especially considering he doesn't even play basketball!

THE NEED FOR SPEED!

Whoosh! There's no substitute for pure lightning strike speed and these guys have all taken the needle into the red with power, guts and a little madness ...

▶ Lightning Bolt

http://y2u.be/4gUW1JikaxQ

"I am trying to be one of the greatest, to be among Ali and Pelé," said Usain Bolt, prior to competing in his final Olympics. That he was going to succeed was never in doubt. Usain Bolt is the fastest human being ever timed, with a list of world records as long as his magnificent, striding legs. At the Rio 2016 games Bolt won gold in the 100 metres, the 200 metres and the 4x100-metre relay. That meant he'd earned three gold medals at three consecutive Olympics and completed a "triple-triple". Truly a living legend.

▶ Car Chase

http://y2u.be/8YcvOsQdi3o

Swedish car manufacturer Koenigsegg's Agera is not just a supercar, it's a hypercar – an elite division of million-dollar, ultra-high-spec sports cars. With big bucks at stake it's a competitive world, so when, in August 2017, Bugatti's Chiron put down a 0–249–0 mph (0–400–0 km/h) record run in 41.96 seconds, Koenigsegg's ears pricked up. In less than a month they sent the Agera out. After a few test runs, the car made the entire run, reaching 250 mph (402 km/h) and coming to a halt in 36.44 seconds over a distance of 1.57 miles (2.52 kilometres).

THE FASTEST 100M SPRINT ON RECORD

▼ Splash Dash

http://y2u.be/sAubG28uODM

As speed records go, driving at 54 mph (87 km/h) isn't very fast. Except Gudbjørn Grimsson is driving on water. In an extreme Formula Offroad race in Iceland, the local driver took his suitably named Insane Racing buggy through the mud and drove over 1,000 feet (300 metres) down the river. With huge-treaded tyres acting like scoops on a paddle steamer, the buggy skims along on the water. To generate enough power, the car has four-wheel drive and a 1,600 horsepower twin-turbo engine. So probably best not to try it in the family estate car then.

THE FASTEST CAR ON WATER

▼ Stop the Clock

http://y2u.be/xG91krXuxyw

"Oh my God! From lane eight, a world record… I have never seen anything from 200 to 400 like that," shouted Michael Johnson as he watched his 400-metre world record change hands in Rio 2016. "That was a massacre from Wayde van Niekerk. He just put those guys away." This was the stand-out athletic performance of the games, as the South African not only shaved 0.15 seconds off a record that had stood since 1999, but also became the first man to win an Olympic 400-metre title from lane 8.

Handstand Finish

http://y2u.be/9p8LZVZoUzk

Tameru Zegeye is known as "The Miracle Man of Ethiopia". Born with deformed feet and unable to use his legs, Tameru learned to walk on his hands. His agility earned him a place in a circus, but he has proved his athletic skills as well. While visiting the small town of Fürth in north Bavaria, Germany, the 32-year-old completed a 100-metre sprint on crutches in a world record time of 56 seconds. What is really amazing is Tameru's technique, an incredible gravity-defying combination of balance, strength and co-ordination.

EXTREME WEATHER

Witness the shock and devastation brought by these record-breaking natural disasters – hurricanes, tsunamis and other calamitous events – in tense and dramatic footage uploaded to YouTube.

▶ Weather Report

http://y2u.be/unV5KcSrY-I

This clip went viral and became known as the 'Hurricane Charley Gas Station' video. It shows a petrol station in Charlotte Harbor, Florida being torn apart by winds of over 155 mph (249 km/h). Hurricane Charley, classed as Category 4 (the second strongest band), was the strongest hurricane to hit southwest Florida for 50 years. These winds were the strongest ever caught on video and were captured by Mike Theiss, whose brilliant weather films appear on the Ultimate Chase channel.

The Super Tsunami

http://y2u.be/yN6EgMMrhdI

On 9 July 1958, an earthquake caused a landslide at the head of Lituya Bay in Alaska. It generated a mega-tsunami measuring between 100 feet (30 metres) and 300 feet (91 metres), the highest tsunami wave in recorded history. This fascinating four-minute BBC clip tells the story of the tsunami, illuminated by the incredible tale of two witnesses, the only survivors from the boats out that day. It has been viewed over 5 million times.

▶ Hailstone from Hell

http://y2u.be/w47HxYgG7bg

The hailstones that fell in Vivian, South Dakota in 2010 weren't unpleasant, they were downright dangerous. As massive ice balls pummelled the ground and houses, locals described it as like having someone throw bricks from an airplane. After the storm, Les Scott picked the largest hailstone to put in his daquiri, then thought better of it. He contacted the National Weather Service who revealed that both the weight – 1.9375 pounds (31 ounces, 880 grams) and the circumference – 18.5 inches (44.5 centimetres) made it a record breaker.

THE LARGEST LANDSLIDE IN HISTORY

▲ Mount Devastation

http://y2u.be/IhU6jml6NY4

Mount St Helens is a volcano in the US state of Washington. In 1980 an earthquake caused the north face to slide away, creating the largest landslide ever recorded. The landslide triggered explosions that sent rocks, ash, volcanic gas and steam into the air at over 300 mph (483 km/h) and created a column of ash that reached more than 15 miles (24 kilometres) into the atmosphere in only 15 minutes. This video, created from a series of photographs, reveals the enormity of this colossal act of nature.

AMAZING ANIMAL RECORDS

The animal kingdom has its champions too. A safari through YouTube's wildlife clips reveals some fascinating and surprising records and some incredible footage from the wild world.

▶ Monkey Business

http://y2u.be/zsXP8qeFF6A

About 98 per cent of their genome is identical to humans, so it is not surprising that chimpanzees are regarded as the cleverest of animal species. They can make and use tools, hunt in organized groups and have shown they are capable of empathy, altruism and self-awareness. Over and above all this, they are adept at computer skills – and in the case of Ayumu, featured in this video, can beat a human at memory games.

CHIMP WITH A MEMORY SUPERIOR TO HuMANS

◀ Big Bug

http://y2u.be/tBaRwtzFBbo

The Maoris call it "the God of Ugly Things". Bit rude? Looking at a picture of the Giant Weta, you might think it's a little like a cricket and not really that unsightly, but see the insect in real life and – whoa! – it's the size of a rodent. Once common in New Zealand, the world's biggest insect is now believed to live only on Little Barrier Island, about 50 miles northeast of Auckland. Weighing more than a sparrow, this creature is too heavy to jump, let alone fly, but it can pack a nasty nip with its oversized pincers.

▼ Don't Have a Cow

http://y2u.be/JMWrXkLGCwA

The world's tallest cow ever officially recorded was Blosom, a female Holstein. She weighed in at a whopping height of 74.8 inches (190 centimetres) – that's over 6 feet tall! Blosom was first recognized by the Guinness World Records in Orangeville, Illinois, USA, in May 2014, but went on to receive another honour, World's Tallest Cow Ever, in 2015.

▲ Dive Bomb

http://y2u.be/r7lgIchYNew

Most people would quickly name the cheetah as the fastest creature on earth, but the fastest creature on the planet? The answer is the Peregrine Falcon. Its horizontal cruising speeds reach to just 50–65 mph (80–100 km/h), but when it is in a hunting dive, known as a stoop, this bird of prey regularly flies over 150 mph (240 km/h), more than twice the speed of the cheetah, and has been recorded at 242 mph (389 km/h). They plunge at such a rate that they usually kill their prey with a single blow.

WORLD'S TALLEST COW

No Slouch

http://y2u.be/rR4L6Gil1AE

"When Bertie gets going, there's no stopping him," the owner of Adventure Valley, a children's park in County Durham, told the *Guardian* newspaper, clearly suspecting that Bertie was the Usain Bolt of the tortoise world, and, indeed, when Bertie was put to the test in September 2015, he smashed the record, covering 18 feet (5.48 metres) in 19.59 seconds. This was twice as fast as the previous time of 43.7 seconds, which had stood since 1977. Bertie's speed equates to sprinting a mighty 0.6 mph (1 km/h), so all hail the fastest tortoise in the world.

FREAKY FOOD RECORDS

The world of food and drink showcases some marvellous records, including enormous vegetables, oversized fast food and a time-honoured crazy method of cracking open champagne bottles.

▶ Burger King

http://y2u.be/KQ0uDYdpHfs

Two all-beef patties, special sauce, lettuce, cheese, pickles, onions – on a sesame seed bun. It's what we all know as a McDonald's Big Mac. And Matt Stonie is going to eat 25 of these? In less than an hour? We're talking around 11 pounds (5 kilos) of fast food, packing a hefty 13,250 calories. Popular YouTuber Matt, however, is nothing if not dedicated to his cause and, after getting over the $120 damage to his credit card at the drive-thru, he settles gamely to the task. Have a look. It's an entertaining watch, but perhaps not best viewed on a full stomach.

Grim Reaper

http://y2u.be/3zhym9oUSGU

The "Carolina Reaper", a crossbreed between a Ghost chilli pepper and a Red Habanero pepper, has been rated as the world's hottest chilli pepper. It averages a 1,569,300 on the Scoville scale, making it over 900 times hotter than Tabasco sauce. There are enough chilli-eating videos on YouTube to show what excruciating results can occur, but despite that the Danish TV host, Bubber, is foolish enough to step up to the plate...

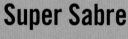

Super Sabre

http://y2u.be/k_vfg1dJito

Napoleon is reputed to have declared: "Champagne! In victory one deserves it; in defeat one needs it." It was his troops who first popularized "sabring" champagne bottles – severing the neck from the bottle with the flat edge of a sabre. It is a precise skill – cutting through the glass at an exact stress point – and is one perfected by Mitch Ancona as he opens a world record 34 bottles in a minute. An achievement worth celebrating.

▼ Onion King

http://y2u.be/ZClfa3L0dtY

Tony Glover was named King of the Onions when he managed to produce a mighty onion weighing 18 pounds 11 ounces (8.5 kilograms). Using seeds bought from the previous record holder, Peter Glazebrook, Tony says it took nearly a year to grow his mighty specimen. He gives them nitrogen-rich food and ensures the humidity is just right. Giant onions have trebled in size since 1985 and word has it that the holy grail of onions – the 20-pounder (9 kilograms) – is just around the corner.

THE WORLD'S LARGEST ONION

◀ Pizza the Action

http://y2u.be/IT09m7mOItM

In front of 6,000 cheering spectators, Pali Grewal, a pizza chef in south London, made three large pizzas in 39.1 seconds – a pizza every 13 seconds. The contestants at the competition had to hand stretch fresh dough, spread the tomato sauce and top three large pizzas – one pepperoni, one mushroom and one cheese. Quality was scrutinized as two judges inspected each aspect of the process. If the pizza was not perfect, it was returned to the competitor to be remade.

THE FASTEST PIZZA MAKER IN THE WORLD

RECORD-BREAKING PEOPLE

Those born at the extremes of the physical spectrum – the tallest, the smallest, etc. – have always held a special fascination. These clips reveal the human beings behind some of the statistics.

▶ A Tall Story

http://y2u.be/RwzMWuAxANw

Robert Pershing Wadlow from Alton, Illinois, USA is the tallest recorded person ever to have lived. He was born in 1918 and by the time he was eight years old he was 6 feet 2 inches (1.88 metres) tall. By the time he was 19 he had reached a height of 8 feet 11.1 inches (2.72 metres) – the tallest living man is a mere 8 feet 1 inch (2.46 metres). Unfortunately, Robert would only live a few years more after an infection in his foot spread to his body. He was known as the Gentle Giant and over 27,000 people attended his funeral.

Towering Teen

http://y2u.be/hBq06yJYqLQ

Teenage growth spurts are a common phenomenon. One minute your nephew is a 4-foot 12-year-old and the next time you see him he's 14 and pushing 6 feet. American Broc Brown is something else, though. Because of a genetic disorder known as Sotos Syndrome, or cerebral gigantism, he's been growing up to 6 inches a year throughout his teens. Broc is now 19 and stands 7 feet 8 inches (2.33 metres) tall. About to leave "teenagerdom" behind, Broc is on course to become the world's tallest man. The current record is held by Turkish farmer Sultan Kosen, who stands at 8 feet 1 inch (2.46 metres).

THE TALLEST MAN WHO EVER LIVED

◀ Animal Magnetism

http://y2u.be/rbUuzCRa3Ug

Former kick-boxing coach Etibar Elchyev from Georgia is known as "Magnetic Man". Ever since he discovered his ability to attract metal objects to his body, Etibar has been setting new records. Here, in December 2013, we find him putting spoons on his chest and back – 53 in total, a new world record. An excellent talent, but he must dread visiting the cafeteria. Scientists claim his skin is not magnetic but merely "sticky". Whatever ... he's still in a magnetic field of his own!

▶ Inseparable Brothers

http://y2u.be/gPcijt2WaIs

Twin brothers Ronnie and Donnie Galyon were born healthy in Dayton, Ohio, in October 1951. Joined at the waist, they each had arms, legs and separate hearts but shared a stomach and some organs. Sixty-three years later they were still joined and could celebrate being the oldest-ever conjoined twins, beating Italian brothers Giacomo and Giovanni Battista Tocci, who were born in 1877. The twins spent their lives from the age of four in circus sideshows but have now retired to live with their younger brother.

THE LONGEST-
LIVING TWINS
IN THE WORLD

WILD AND WACKY

Hidden away in the nooks and corners of YouTube are some odd and eccentric records. Here are just a few ...

◢ Living Doll

http://y2u.be/mhcW_81GRsU

Now aged 33, Brazilian-born Briton Rodrigo Alves has been having cosmetic surgery for over 15 years. He has had 51 surgeries and more than 100 cosmetic procedures – an official world record – and has completely changed his appearance. His nickname is "Human Ken" (after Barbie's boyfriend) and he most recently underwent a CO_2 laser treatment that burned off the top layer of his skin to leave him with a porcelain-like, blemish-free complexion. Alves, who is set to appear in a TV series about real-life dolls, says he has no intention of stopping and plans even more cosmetic changes.

THE WORLD'S MOST DOLL-LIKE HUMAN

Cup Winner

http://y2u.be/RsBdA2S2E-8

Sport stacking is a game in which competitors stack plastic cups in specific sequences as quickly as possible. The toughest of the disciplines is the "cycle" in which 12 cups are stacked in three different ways, including pyramid formations. Fifteen-year-old William Orrell is the indisputable king of stacking – holding the record for all three individual disciplines. This clip shows his incredible record-breaking cycle stack at the first-ever Nation's Capital Open Sport Stacking Tournament where he takes just 5.1 seconds to finish.

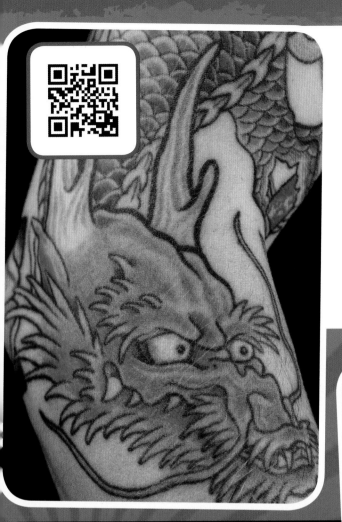

◀ Tattoo Love

http://y2u.be/QlULSyKlrGY

Couples need a shared interest and there's no prize for guessing Chuck Helmke and Charlotte Guttenberg's common passion. Chuck, aged 75, and Charlotte, a sprightly 65-year-old, met in a tattoo studio in 2006. Charlotte was just discovering the joys of body art, while Chuck had begun covering his body in ink five years earlier. Now they are officially the male and female most-tattooed senior citizens world record holders. Displaying a colourful array of intricate tattoos, both boast over 90 per cent body coverage, with even their shaved heads inked. There's not a lot anyone can do to beat that!

MOST-TATTOOED SENIOR CITIZENS

▶ Dead Cool

http://y2u.be/xtHzRjnoXKw

In November 2014 in Mexico City, 509 slightly scary-looking skeletons in ball gowns and brimmed hats gathered in the city centre to set the world record for the largest gathering of Catrinas. The figure of Catrina, known as the Elegant Death, was created and immortalized in works by artists Guadalupe Posada and Diego Rivera and is now a traditional part of Mexico's Day of the Dead celebrations. People dress as the skeletal character to visit cemeteries and share offerings and food with the dead and their families.

A RECORD GATHERING OF CATRINAS

SPORTS RECORD BREAKERS

There's more to sport than winning. There are records to be broken. These athletes have etched their names in the history of their sports – however strange!

▶ All in a Day's Work

http://y2u.be/CQIk-aAHhFY

These days, breaking a record is as much about producing a great YouTube video as it is about performing the feat. The Face Team Acrobatic Sports Theatre of Hungary have certainly grasped that fact. They broke five world records in one day – the most basketball slam dunks by a team using a trampoline in one minute; the highest throw and catch of a spinning basketball; the farthest forward flip trampette slam dunk; the longest time spinning a basketball on a guitar; and the most passes of a spinning basketball in one minute (pair) – and captured it all in a fun three-minute video. Perfect.

Xtreme 19th

http://y2u.be/iOWR7O1oSgU

The Legend Golf 18-hole course in South Africa has a bonus hole – the "Xtreme 19th" – the highest and longest par three golf hole in the world. The tee sits on top of a cliff on Hanglip Mountain, more than 1,400 feet (427 metres) above a green carved in the shape of the continent of Africa – it takes nearly 30 seconds for the ball to hit the ground. Drill a hole-in-one and you win $1 million, but no one has yet bettered a two-shot birdie.

BEST LEAPING BASKET-BALLERS

◄ Skyfall

http://y2u.be/2YSQ7-e-fZ0

In December 2016, Arsenal teammates Laurent Koscielny, Francis Coquelin, Theo Walcott and Nacho Monreal each attempted to break the record for the highest-altitude football dropped and controlled. It was England forward Theo Walcott who showed the necessary skill, not only bringing a ball dropped from a height of 111.5 feet (34 metres) under control first time, but also keeping it off the ground for four further touches. It's not a tactic the Gunners have employed before, but if you see them launching the ball skywards in a future game, you know just who they expect to be underneath it.

Golf War

http://y2u.be/5ZkbL_qZRE0

Golf is a sedate game, played at walking pace. You have time to consider each shot carefully. Usually. Except the European Tour turned things on their head by organising a Fastest Hole of Golf by a Team of Four competition. Under floodlights on the 503-yard (457-metre), par-five 15th hole at the Regnum Carya resort in Turkey, holders Team France defended their title against Team England and Team South Africa. Allowed one shot each in relay, the four-man teams were up against a long fairway, a water hazard and a stopwatch – and it was a nail-biter…

► Clogged Up

http://y2u.be/2CdYF41M6rw

Australian Rugby Union hero Drew Mitchell is his country's highest World Cup try scorer. However, the Toulon winger, who has played over 70 times for Australia, is also a serial record breaker. On the Sky Sports Rugby TV channel, he became joint holder of the records for both the most rugby passes and the most drop goals in a minute. He then set the record for the most apples crushed with the bicep in one minute (it was 14) and went on to perform this intriguing feat: the fastest 100 metres in clogs. Wearing the heavy wooden, Klomp-style clog common to the Netherlands, Drew hit the finish line in just 14.43 seconds.

FASTEST 100M WEARING CLOGS

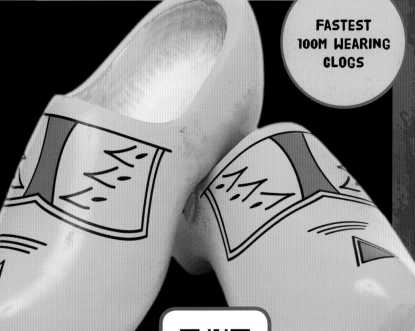

THEME PARK RECORDS

Scream if you want to go faster! Actually, it isn't possible to go any faster than on some of these record-breaking rides – but you may find yourself screaming anyway.

FASTEST, LONGEST, TALLEST DIVE COASTER

Scream Machine

http://y2u.be/6EjSI_FKDBY

Cedar Point in Sandusky, Ohio, seems determined to retain its reputation as the rollercoaster capital of the world. Its 2016 summer addition, Valravn, is the tallest (223 feet/68 metre), fastest (75 mph/120 km/h) and longest (3,415 feet/1,040 metre) dive coaster in the world. As this terrifying frontseat POV shows, it climbs to give riders a superb view of Lake Erie before the fun begins. They are then sent on a 214-foot (65-metre), 90-degree free-fall, before a loop-the-loop section that turns them upside down three times. Hands up, who's ready to go round again?

▼ Gee Force

http://y2u.be/N79JKDtK4hg

What is it with you people? Sixteen million views? It's just a ride! The Zumanjaro: Drop of Doom, at the Six Flags Great Adventure in New Jersey, USA, is the tallest and fastest drop ride in the world. The eight-person gondola speeds to the top of the 415-foot (126-metre) structure in about 30 seconds, leaves them there a while to enjoy the view (or just exchange some nervous giggles) before rocketing them back down at 90 mph (145 km/h), reaching ground level again in less than 10 seconds – before they even have time to scream.

THE WORLD'S FASTEST DROP RIDE

▼ Vomit Comet

http://y2u.be/qqN9PDS3hOc

People have been known to queue for over four hours to ride for just 2 minutes, 45 seconds on the Smiler at Alton Towers, a theme park in the UK. It is the rollercoaster with the most inversions (turning riders upside down and back again) in the world. There are 14 different inversions of seven different kinds from the common corkscrew, cobra and dive-loops to the rarer double batwing and sea-serpent twists. Confused? Never mind, climb aboard and hold tight!

Fast Formula

http://y2u.be/ijuQwnfBBZw

The Formula Rossa rollercoaster in Abu Dhabi's Ferrari World boasts acceleration from 0 to 60 mph (96 km/h) in just two seconds and reaches a world record 149 mph (240 km/h). In 2010, Felipe Massa and Fernando Alonso, Formula One motor-racing drivers, took their seats in the fastest rollercoaster on the planet. Now, while their bodies are used to being flung around at ridiculously high speeds, their faces are usually encased in helmets. Just watch as the G-force hits these seasoned speed merchants.

RECORD-BREAKING TWISTS ON A ROLLER-COASTER

SCARY AND SHOCKING!

Delve into the lucky dip of the world of records and who knows what'll emerge. You could find some hair-raising danger, interesting collections and, sometimes, something truly, truly bizarre.

DEATH ROAD – WORLD'S MOST DANGEROUS

▲ Rocky Road

http://y2u.be/zGA3qXQs1wE

The North Yungas Road in Bolivia is 43 miles (69 kilometres) long and 2,000 feet (610 metres) high, and claims around 300 lives a year. No wonder it is called the Death Road. Perils along the Most Dangerous Road in the World include rock avalanches, fog and trucks squeezing by each other on its loose-stone surface. Often a single track 10 feet (3 metres) wide, it has no guard rails, just sheer drops down the cliff edges. The route does, however, offer some stunning scenery.

▼ Selfie-Made Man

http://y2u.be/ClGajvF89NQ

In February 2016, at the *Zoolander 2* premiere in Leicester Square, Hollywood star Ben Stiller set a world record for the longest selfie-stick picture. His snap featured members of the cast, including co-stars Penelope Cruz and Clive Owen. Less than a month later, London-based YouTuber James Ware constructed a 31-foot (9.57-metre) stick – a whole three feet bigger than Ben's. As he attempted his shot, James was moved on from Trafalgar Square by an irate security guard and had to settle for a less-celebrated background. His selfie has no stars, just a bemused passer-by, but no one ever said records have to be glamorous.

Walk the Plank

http://y2u.be/KbtZfzxX44o

How far are you prepared to go for a breathtaking view? If you would happily walk along a seemingly rickety plank attached to the side of a mountain cliff hundreds of feet high, then Mount Hua in China could be your ideal destination. The plankway doesn't lead anywhere – just to a stunning bird's-eye view of the surrounding mountains – and you have to return the same way, negotiating your way past those coming in the opposite direction. Overcome your fears, though, and you, too, can claim to have taken the world's most dangerous hiking trail.

Human Fireball

http://y2u.be/hICWU9HC7ts

Fire-protective clothing is available. It's worn by motor-racing drivers and movie stunt men. It's not for Anthony Britton, though. He dressed himself in three pairs of overalls, a few balaclavas and a motorcycle helmet for his attempt on the world record for fire running. Hundreds of spectators assembled in a park in Croydon, England, to watch Anthony, an experienced escapologist, soak himself in petrol, set himself on fire and run hell for leather across the grass. He completed an awesome 595 feet (181 metres) before calling in his team to douse the flames with fire extinguishers.

▶ Blown Away

http://y2u.be/AdtSdVop6V0

The James Bond franchise of movies has a long history of breaking a plethora of records. However, its latest achievement is arguably the most earth-shattering of them all. The climax of *Spectre*, the 24th Bond film in the series, featured the largest film-stunt explosion ever as Blofeld's desert base was detonated to kingdom come in front of the film's stars, Daniel Craig and Madeleine Swann. Shot on 29 June 2015 in Erfoud, Morocco, the blast used 2,224 gallons of fuel and 73 pounds (33 kilograms) of explosives. The sequence might have lasted just seven and a half seconds, but it was one memorable blast.

DON'T TRY THIS AT HOME!

How desperate can you be to get your name in the record books? These record breakers seem to feel no pain as they take one or more of their senses to the limit.

Candles in the Wind

http://y2u.be/kvGa-OXORhw

It's not big and it's not clever – though you have to admit it is kind of cool. File this in the not-to-try-at-home folder, but do take a look at 28-year-old Filipino Ronald Cabañas extinguishing 5 lit candles with his own bottom wind. In an extraordinary display of controlled flatulence, Ronald, using what can only be described as a home-made fart trumpet, puts out the candles in less than 30 seconds. It is a fine skill, but it's difficult to see how Ronald, a farmer and sometime porter, can make a career of it.

▶ Peg Face

http://y2u.be/pS2AszO0z44

We've all got a skill lurking somewhere, it's just a matter of finding it. Kelvin "The Peg Man" Mercado, 36 years old, discovered he had a unique talent for clipping clothes pegs on his face. Now he's a world-record holder. Pegs are attached in neat formation to every loose, and not so loose, piece of skin as well as to his lips and nose. Altogether he managed to clip on 163 pegs – and it makes for quite a sight.

GREATEST NUMBER OF PEGS ON FACE

▼ Saucy Drinker

http://y2u.be/Q60mABHsSxM

The bartender in *Back to the Future Part III* refers to it as 'wake-up juice', but just the sight of the familiar jar of Tabasco sauce is enough to strike fear into the heart of many a diner. Its three simple ingredients - red peppers, salt and distilled vinegar - pack a punch measuring 2,500–5,000 SHU on the Scoville scale. Hats off then to Andrew Hajinikitas who is prepared to risk his dignity by downing two bottles in 30 seconds live on television!

Ay, Caramba!

http://y2u.be/LuNmbW-VQyQ

How many characters from *The Simpsons* cartoon series can you name? A look at Michael Baxter's shoulder will help. The 52-year-old Australian has a record 203 characters from the cartoon show tattooed on his back. The family, of course, are drawn largest, but minor characters, from Sideshow Bob to Kent Brockman, all get inked in. Over the course of a year, the prison officer sat through an eye-watering 130 hours under the needle, but he had his record confirmed in time to celebrate the series' 25th anniversary.

▶ Ring of Fire

http://y2u.be/F--nCc58sTc

At South Africa's largest gathering of motorcyclists, known as the "Rhino Rally", on 5 September 2014, petrol-heads Enrico Schoeman and André de Kock turned up the heat for their next record-breaking feat – riding a bright pink motorcycle and sidecar through a burning tunnel of fire and flames 395 feet (120.4 metres) long! Afterwards, driver Enrico Schoeman admitted, "I was so disoriented by the heat, I couldn't see where I was going." Crikey!

LONGEST MOTORCYCLE RUN THROUGH TUNNEL OF FIRE

THIRST-QUENCHING RECORDS

It's not just drinking the liquid stuff quickly (although, boy, can they guzzle!), but shaking it, sucking it, carrying it and performing all sorts of records with it!

Beer Duty

http://y2u.be/nALw8IOLDfw

Tax inspector by day, tankard carrier by beer festival, Oliver Strümpfel is a superhero in the bar-tending world. His personal arena is the Gillamoos Fair in Abensberg, Bavaria, where he is king of the *Maßkrugtragen* – the beer-stein carrying challenge. He took up the challenge to try to beat an Australian who reigned as the Meister of *Maßkrugtragen*. In 2010 he managed to beat him by carrying 21 tankards. In 2014 he took his record to 25. Following a nine-month gym regime, this is Strümpfel's 2017 attempt to extend his record even further.

A Splash of Cola

http://y2u.be/uQ05eALMBEo

As every schoolchild knows, Mentos and cola make for the best science lesson ever. No one remembers the point, but if all goes well they create a terrific fountain. Over 500 Cincinnatians gathered in the city's Fountain Square in 2007 to launch the largest number of Mentos Geysers to be set off at once in one location. The splash-off was synchronized, leading to a fabulous spray of cola – and a sticky mess in the middle of town.

▶ Flip Out

http://y2u.be/INb2FChnoIQ

As 2017 began, bottle-flipping had reached epidemic proportions. Kids everywhere were flicking a partially filled plastic bottle in the hope it would land on its base. Schools banned the practice and Mike Senatore, the man whose viral video had launched the craze, went online to apologise for distracting the nation's youth. Out in Sweden, things became even crazier. With a 130-litre bottle supplied by supermarket chain Lidl, two YouTubers ventured to the middle of a bridge to attempt the world's biggest bottle flip...

CHAMPION BOTTLE-FLIPPER

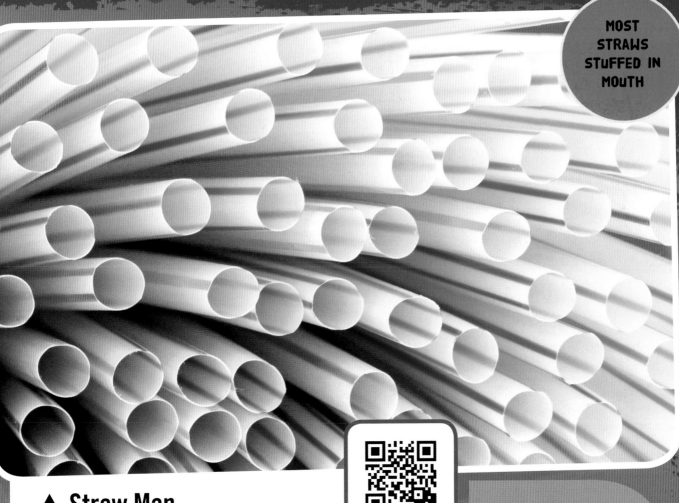

▲ Straw Man

http://y2u.be/15BCllVcz38

As a child, Manoj Kumar Maharana dreamed of breaking a world record and, finally, as a 23-year-old, he fulfilled his ambition. He could have set out to win the Olympic 100 Metres or lift a car above his head, but instead he decided to beat Simon Elmore, a Brit who crammed 400 straws in his mouth in 2009. In 2017, Manoj managed to stuff an amazing 459 plastic drinking straws into his mouth at once, successfully keeping them there for the requisite 10 seconds without touching them.

▼ Milking It

http://y2u.be/kBFugzV1KxI

Kobayashi (also see page 107) shows his awesome power of consumption. Here he is at Uncle Bob's Self Storage in Upper Saddle River, New Jersey, tipping a gallon – that's eight pints! – of milk down his gullet in just 20 seconds. According to the clip's description, Kobayashi had set a record of eating 13 cupcakes in a minute, "so he needed to wash it down". Considering human stomachs are said to be able to contain around six pints, it's difficult to imagine where it is all going.

Human Hydrant

http://y2u.be/U9_JFjZGkYA

There are over 600 muscles in the human body and many of them can be utilised to break a world record. Take Kirubel Yilma of Addis Ababa for example. He's a medical student who put his knowledge of anatomy to use to achieve a record for spraying water from the mouth. He beat the existing record by 10 seconds as he squirted a continuous spray of water from his mouth for nearly a minute!

THE BIGGEST!

When it comes to record breaking, size is definitely important. The Biggest ... is always one of the most popular of the records categories. Here are a few colossal contributors ...

Right on Cue

http://y2u.be/dy6wkqRzc5I

When French billiards player Florian "Venom Trickshots" Kohler turned up in Las Vegas with a pool cue that was 17 feet and 7.4 inches (5.37 metres) long, he could hardly get it in the room. There was no doubt it was the longest pool cue ever but, to gain the record, Florian had to prove he could use it by breaking (splitting) the balls and then potting seven of them. As the weight of the cue was making it sag and bend in the middle, to secure that record the master player was going to have to use every last one of his silky skills...

THE LARGEST LEGO STRUCTURE

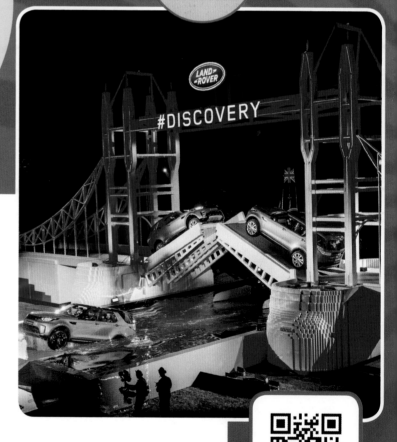

▶ Tower of Power

http://y2u.be/kQh9ommsWFk

Remember how pleased you felt when you built your first Lego house? With about 300 or so pieces? Here's the record largest Lego structure. This giant replica of London's Tower Bridge was constructed over five months and needed nearly six million Lego bricks (laid end to end, the bricks would stretch from Tower Bridge all the way to Paris). The model was made to help celebrate the latest Land Rover Discovery, which drove across the bridge. But, for many, the steel-strengthened 42-foot (13-metre) plastic structure was the star of the show.

Big Game Boy

http://y2u.be/ezHsGggQEDg

The Nintendo Game Boy was a 1990s must-have device. This handheld console was the only way to play *Tetris* or *Super Mario* on the move. So forget your Xbox or PS4 – who wouldn't want a human-sized Game Boy? Belgian engineering student Ilhan Unal has entered the record books for creating the largest, fully functional Game Boy. The 21-year-old designed the giant console on his computer and then spent a month in a laboratory building it before wiring it to a normal Game Boy to enable it to play the original.

▼ Off the Wall

http://y2u.be/EptwF6cZMWg

Of all the records set in Brazil's Olympic year, this is the most eye-catching. Artist Eduardo Kobra designed a huge mural called *Etnias*, meaning "Ethnicities", on a wall of the Olympic Boulevard in Rio de Janeiro. The colourful spray-painted mural depicts the faces of indigenous people from five different continents. Using 180 buckets of acrylic paint and 3,500 cans of spray paint, the painting stands 51 feet (15.5 metres) high and stretches for 560 feet (170 metres). It's the largest spray-painted mural in the world, and it took Kobra and his team two months to complete.

THE WORLD'S BIGGEST MURAL

THE MORE, THE MERRIER!

Ah, mass participation! A chance to meet other bizarrely dressed folk, to stretch your legs in unison or to smack each other around the head with a pillow!

▼ Zombie Apocalypse (almost)

http://y2u.be/QkqC6Fni2KE

They bill the Zombie Pub Crawl as the World's Greatest Undead Party with brain-eating competitions, live pop acts, a "Trapped in the Closet Sing-Along" and a zombie fun run! Minneapolis has been hosting the living dead (or people dressed up as them) annually since 2005. The original 500 zombies have multiplied until, in 2014, over 15,000 people were officially counted stumbling around in a stupefied manner. It was the official record for a zombie gathering.

RECORD-BREAKING NUMBER OF ZOMBIES

▲ Pillow Talk

http://y2u.be/KQ_SYl9vlkc

Nobody wants to see fighting at a sports stadium, but maybe we can make an exception for CHS Field, the home of Minnesota baseball team St Paul Saints. At the end of the second inning of the Saints' match against the Winnipeg Goldeyes, a battle broke out – among all 6,261 of the spectators. This was a mass display of that friendliest of confrontations – the pillow fight. Provided with weapons by a local pillow company, the crowd, staff and mascots (although sadly not the players) attacked their neighbours with their night-time bolsters. It was the biggest pillow fight in the world – ever!

▶ Keeping the Peace

http://y2u.be/CLz_txJFqNw

There are always a fair few peace signs in evidence at the Glastonbury music festival, but never anything as massive as this. Long associated with the Campaign for Nuclear Disarmament, the festival organisers are keen to spread the message of world peace. So, in 2017, in the wake of terrorist attacks in Manchester and London, they decided to send out their own message of unity. Around 15,000 people – some of them witnesses of those attacks – gathered at Glastonbury's monumental stone circle to form the largest ever human peace sign.

LARGEST HUMAN PEACE SIGN

◣ Packed Pillion

http://y2u.be/YwRafRr8dk4

The Indian Army has set a new world record for 58 men riding on a single motorbike. It's not a skill modern soldiers should need but, with defence-budget cuts common, you never know. The 500-cc Royal Enfield chugged along an Air Force runway and covered a distance of 0.75 miles (1.2 kilometres) with members of the Tornadoes, an army motorcycle display team, precariously balancing on either side. The stunt, which broke the Tornadoes' own record by four riders, involved six months' planning and training, military discipline and precision – and quite a lot of falling off.

MOST PEOPLE RIDING A SINGLE MOTORBIKE

Yo Ho Whoa!

http://y2u.be/uoW2A_vqwpQ

Santa Claus traditionally sails through the air on his reindeer-pulled sleigh. Well, not in Bondi Beach in Sydney, Australia, he doesn't. In the world-famous surfing resort, Father Christmas comes ashore on a surfboard – and not just one, but hundreds of them! In December 2015, 320 surfing Santas broke the world record for the largest surf lesson. In their red suits and (some) white beards, the Santas took part in a day-long surfing masterclass in aid of a local charity. So, if your presents don't arrive this Christmas, maybe Santa's still catching a wave out in Bondi.

WILD WEATHER RECORDS

Mother Nature is a prodigious record breaker and produces some of the most spectacular events you can see on YouTube. Just watch the disintegrating iceberg, dramatic twister and other gripping footage on these pages.

Tip of the Iceberg

http://y2u.be/hC3VTglPoGU

Over 20 million people have watched this amazing clip from the documentary *Chasing Ice*. The footage shows the historic breakup at the Ilulissat Glacier in western Greenland – the largest iceberg calving ever filmed. Glacial calving happens when an iceberg breaks off from the larger ice shelf, in this case a piece measuring 1.8 cubic miles (7.4 cubic kilometres). The Ilulissat (aka Jakobshavn) glacier produces around 10 per cent of all Greenland icebergs with around 35 billion tonnes of icebergs calving off every year.

It's a Twister!

http://y2u.be/Q7X3fyId2U0

During the evening of 31 May 2013, the widest tornado in recorded history occurred over rural areas of central Oklahoma. It was 2.6 miles (4.2 kilometres) wide at its widest point and tracked across 16.2 miles (26 kilometres). The storm, with accompanying wind speeds of more than 295 mph (475 km/h), fortunately struck mostly in rural areas. Even so, eight people lost their lives as a result of the tornado. All of them were killed in vehicles – either they were trying to flee by outdriving the twister or they were storm chasers filming the cataclysmic event.

THE WIDEST TORNADO EVER RECORDED

RECORD-BREAKING LIGHTNING STORMS

▲ Everlasting Lightning

http://y2u.be/edrAL2t99kE

In 2014, an area of northwestern Venezuela, where the Catatumbo River meets Lake Maracaibo, was officially recognized as having the most frequent lightning storms. Known as Relámpago del Catatumbo – the Catatumbo Lightning – this "everlasting storm" appears almost every night. Averaging 28 lightning strikes per minute for up to 10 hours at a time, it can spark as many as 3,600 bolts in an hour. Although many myths surround the phenomenon, scientists claim it is just regular lightning, whose frequency can be explained by regional topography and wind patterns.

Chillsville, Siberia

http://y2u.be/gRbaAaJgW0A

Next time you feel a little chilly, spare a thought for the 500 or so inhabitants of Oymyakon, the coldest inhabited place on Earth. Oymyakon (the name ironically means "unfrozen water") is in north-eastern Siberia, a two-day drive from the world's coldest major city, Yakutsk, and just a few hundred miles from the Arctic Circle. It is pitch-black dark for up to 21 hours a day during the winter and the temperature averages -50° Celsius (-58° Fahrenheit). In 1933, it plunged to -68°C (-90°F). Get through that, though, and you can look forward to endless summer days and temperatures rising to a balmy 23°Celsius (73.4°F).

Magma Mia

http://y2u.be/888nbjvkNts

Kilauea, the world's most active volcano, has been erupting on a continuous basis since 1983, but it's been active for over 200,000 years. Its name means "spewing" in the Hawaiian language. It is a shield-type volcano that makes up the south-eastern side of the Big Island of Hawaii, rising 4,190 feet (1,227 metres) above sea level. The latest eruptions have seen the 900° Celsius (1,650° Fahrenheit) lava flow at a rate of 15–20 yards (13.7–18.2 metres) an hour and destroy more than 200 local structures.

EXTREME SPORTS RECORDS

There's danger out there on the streets. Especially if you are mad enough to try to go faster, higher, lower than anyone else in your chosen extreme sport.

Sacré Bleu!

http://y2u.be/8CJURZ5HAs4

French athlete Taig Khris is a hero of the inline skating world but is as well-known by the French public for skating off tall buildings. Having taken a plunge from the first floor of the Eiffel Tower in 2010, Khris now jumped from the Sacré-Coeur – the highest point in Paris. He flew down the 492-foot (150-metre) ramp, taking off with the whole city behind him, and soft-landed on an inflatable half-pipe. He set a new world distance record with a long jump of 95 feet (290 metres).

▶ Surf's Up and Up

http://y2u.be/mLH8OFLclsU

Taking place on International Surfing Day to promote Huntington Beach, California, USA, as *the* Surf City, 66 surf-mad record breakers (aged between 15 and 79) braved the waters on a super-sized (12.83 metres long, 3.37 metres wide) surfboard – so enormous that it had to be lifted into the sea by a forklift truck – to smash the world record for the most people surfing on the same surfboard. The gang of 66 stayed onboard for an impressive 13 seconds to break the record before wiping out.

MOST PEOPLE RIDING THE WORLD'S LARGEST SURFBOARD

◀ Russian BASE Jumper

http://y2u.be/oQjp0DgqWpg

Russian extreme-sports star Valery Rozov endured a 31-day expedition to reach the site of his record-breaking BASE jump. In 2013, he had performed the highest-ever BASE jump on Mount Everest, but that wasn't enough for the adrenaline junkie. In 2016, he climbed to just below the summit of the sixth-highest mountain in the world, Cho Oyu in China, in an attempt to better his record. From a height of over 25,000 feet (7,700 metres), Valery leaped off the mountain, spending 90 seconds in free-fall before his parachute opened, and landing on a glacier 5,500 feet (1,700 metres) below and 11,500 feet (3,500 metres) away.

100-Foot Backflip

http://y2u.be/N93aKejme5I

"I was like, 'Holy moly, I forgot how long I'd be in the air,'" daredevil Cam Zink told ESPN after his monumental 100-foot (30.48-metre) backflip in California in 2014 . "Man, I'm just staring in the sky for like ever." The daredevil hit 46 mph (74 km/h) going downhill before he took off on the world's longest dirt-to-dirt mountain bike backflip and then made a perfect landing. Cam compared his 100-foot breakthrough to the four-minute mile, expecting others to soon take the record further. We'll see ...

▼ Back-Breaking Work

http://y2u.be/Z-OsL4eCgP0

Records don't just happen. New Zealand's Jed Mildon not only spent three intensive months training for his historic triple BMX backflip, but also had to build a super-ramp, 66 feet (20.12 metres) high, into a hillside in order to do it. Jed had kept his attempt to become the first-ever rider to perform three full backwards rotations secret before attempting it in front of 2,000 spectators. They watched spellbound as he careered down the long ramp, shot up a 11.8-foot (3.6-metre) super-kicker, became airborne and created history.

RECORD TRIPLE BACKFLIP

▼ Real-life Iron Man

http://y2u.be/VBTdxGQnWTM

British inventor Richard Browning admits to having had his share of Tony Stark-style control issues with his prototypes, but he's certainly going places with his flying suit. Attaching kerosene-fuelled micro gas turbines – tiny plane engines – to the arms and back of his exo-skeleton suit, he was able to set the first world record for the fastest speed in a body-controlled jet-engine power suit. He only hit speeds of 32.02 mph (51.53 km/h) as he zoomed over Lagoona Park in Reading, UK, but we surely haven't seen the last of this real-life Iron Man.

FASTEST
JET-ENGINE
POWER SUIT

SUPER SPORTS STARS

You don't have to be a big-time pro to be a sporting record breaker. A former NASA scientist, a teenage cheerleader and 6,000 students all wrote their name in the book in style.

Skipping Schoolboy

http://y2u.be/_2y24qfzxGA

It's skipping – but not as you know it. There are no rhyming songs for 15-year-old Cen Xiaolin to jump along to as he competes in the World Inter School Rope Skipping Championships in Dubai. Well, nobody could sing that fast anyway. The high-school student from China's Guangdong Province clocked up a sensational 110 alternate foot skips in 30 seconds and 548 in 3 minutes at the championships. The footage is astonishing – it looks sped up and the rope is virtually invisible, but Cen's hands and legs really are moving that fast.

WORLD'S LARGEST DODGEBALL GAME

▼ University Challenge

http://y2u.be/ZdkU4oDcp40

Forget Oxford and Cambridge or Harvard and Yale; the greatest university rivalry is between the University of California in Irvine and the University of Alberta in Canada. Since 2010, the two colleges have had a running battle to seal the record for the largest dodgeball game. Alberta were the first to make a mark with 1,198 players but since then the honours have swung back and forth. In 2012, in a game involving 6,084 participants, Irvine took the title, but who knows what the Canadians have planned?

Wet the Baby's Head

http://y2u.be/wBsJcGpZvw0

Zyla can't walk or talk, but looks pretty comfortable on water skis. Perhaps that's unsurprising, as she's the daughter of champion barefoot water-skier Keith St Onge and champion show skier Lauren Lane St Onge, but what is surprising is that she's only six months old. Having seen her take to the specially made "baby ski", which they dragged her round the house on, her mum and dad were confident she could actually ski on water – and they were right. In May 2016, Zyla water-skied on Lake Silver, in Winter Haven, Florida, and the proud parents celebrated by posting the video on YouTube.

Tumble Turn

http://y2u.be/deJcMFDMjk0

You may not have heard of Angel Rice but, if power tumbling succeeds in becoming an Olympic sport, she will be a global celebrity. Power tumbling involves momentum and strength in a short series of twists and flips, and the 17-year-old is the USA team's star turn. Known as the "Queen of Tumbling", Angel has twice won the World Cheerleading Championships, but it has been her TV appearances that have brought her the most attention. After breaking the world record for tumbling in one minute on the *Today* show, she was up to her twisting tricks again with Steve Harvey.

▲ Putting It Right

http://y2u.be/htmbMSRj1SQ

Dave Pelz quit being a NASA scientist in 1976 to concentrate on his golf coaching. Using scientific methods, he became an expert in the "short game" – shots made from within around 100 yards of the hole. In 2004, his research paid off. Filming a TV segment for the Golf Channel during PGA Championship week at Whistling Straits in Kohler, Wisconsin, Pelz holed a 206-foot (62.79-metre) putt – beating broadcaster Terry Wogan's previous record of 33 yards (30.2 metres) at Gleneagles.

HIGHEST BASKET EVER MADE

◄ Thunder Strikes Again

http://y2u.be/Wnz4ok5GkZg

Harlem Globetrotters' Thunder Law is the team's designated record-breaker. Longest backwards shot (see page 54), longest basketball shot blindfolded, longest shot while sitting, and now highest upwards shot records have all fallen to the 6 feet and 3 inches (1.905-metre) tall player sporting the number 34. His latest entry in the record books came in 2017 in front of the grand staircase at the Utah State Capitol in Salt Lake City. A hoop was hung from a crane at a height of 50 feet and 1 inch (15.27 metres) and the result was surely never in doubt.

PURE STRENGTH

You won't see weights being lifted like this down the local gym. These guys pull, flip and lift in eye-watering feats of strength that just don't seem possible.

What a Waist

http://y2u.be/jcqRPdvb18w

Paul "Dizzy Hips" Blair. His name kind of gives it away, because Paul is a "hulaholic" – a man addicted to spinning hoops around his waist. Among his extensive collection of world records are the most hoops twirling at once from a dead start (132), twirling the largest hula hoop (43 feet/13.2 metres) and hula hooping for the longest distance (1 mile/1.6 kilometres). This video sees him add brute strength to his unquestionable hula-hooping credentials as he secures the record for the heaviest hula hoop by continuously twirling a 100-pound (45-kilogram) tractor tyre around his waist for over 10 seconds.

Hook, Line and Sinker

http://y2u.be/WgGg0innugM

You don't get given the nickname "The Human Toolbox" for nothing. Among his sword-swallowing and bed-of-nails stunts, extreme entertainer Brad Byers is also given to inserting various items – nails, drill bits, hooks – into his head, usually through the nasal cavity. So, here's a warning: if you are squeamish, this video might not be for you. We see Brad insert a hook and pull along a full multi-person bicycle weighing nearly a ton. It's an obscure record but a mighty impressive one: The Heaviest Load Pulled from a Hook in the Head!

EXTREME HOOK INSERTIONS

THE WOMAN WHOSE STRENGTH IS HER HAIR

▼ Steel Yourself

http://y2u.be/k9rQAOp3xVQ

Amandeep Singh is the Indian Man of Steel – a guy who has immense body strength, seemingly feels no pain and is surely as mad as a box of frogs. Witness his show reel, where he makes his bid to be known as the World's Strongest Man. It's difficult not to wince as he retains a grip on ropes holding back 20 motorcyclists,

has a car run over his head and a full-sized truck run over his rear, and takes sledgehammer blows to his most sensitive body parts. Now that's gotta hurt!

A Smashing Time

http://y2u.be/LqisPXXqpEY

What do you do with those pumpkins once Halloween is over? It isn't a problem for Conor Murphy and his trusty tool. Watch him take a sledge hammer to a truckload of pumpkins; there is something immensely satisfying in such wanton destruction. The CrossFit coach from Boston, USA, makes swift work of pumpkin obliteration as he pounds his way through a record 30 orange gourds in just one minute. It's no mean feat. The guy is seriously fit and he not only secured the world record, but doubled the previous total. Now, who's for pumpkin soup?

▼ Letting Her Hair Down

http://y2u.be/YoBFYQiOCHE

Circus of Horrors star Anastasia IV (Joanna Sawicka from Wimbledon, London) is proud of her hair. She combs it for hours and washes it five times a day. Anastasia isn't vain, she needs to do this to keep her record-breaking hair in top condition. Anastasia spends most of her stage show dangling from her hair, but also lifts record weights with her locks, lifts people, and, in this clip, pulls a 2.5-ton funeral hearse 65 feet 6 inches (20 metres) down the road in under four minutes.

▼ Boeing, Boeing, Gone

http://y2u.be/tls-Jli6eQE

Mark Kirsch is the guy you want on your tug-of-war team. His claims to be the World's Strongest Man of all time look pretty impressive if this clip is anything to go by. We see Mark dragging a Boeing 767 along the runway. Yes! Taxiing a jumbo jet weighing 200,000 pounds (90,720 kilograms) with just a rope and a harness! By hauling the metal monster 100 feet (30.48 metres) in under 40 seconds, he set the world record for the heaviest-ever plane pull.

THE MAN WHO DRAGGED A BOEING

BACKWARDS RECORDS

Doing something backwards is a favourite among record breakers. Sometimes skilful, sometimes dangerous and often looking rather silly, our heroes set to their task without fear of neck ache ...

◀ Thunder's Back

http://y2u.be/o4fzSkAgNP4

Although it has since been broken, Thunder Law of the Harlem Globetrotters used to hold the record for the longest-ever basketball shot. And although he has had to give up that crown, he can take solace in an even more incredible achievement: the longest shot facing away from the hoop. His one-handed backward launch propelled the ball 82 feet and 2 inches (25.04 metres) – almost the length of the court and 10 feet (3.04 metres) further than the previous record – for a perfect three-pointer.

◢ Parallel Parking

http://y2u.be/VSp1olKp_f0

Try this manoeuvre when you're faced with a tight parking space at the local supermarket car park. In front of a live audience at the 2015 Performance Car Show, British stunt driver Alastair Moffatt slid a Fiat 500 1.2 Cult into the narrowest of parallel-parking spaces. Moffat's magnificent handbrake turn was made in a standard car with an enhanced steering wheel and pumped-up tyre pressures. Sliding into a space just 3 inches (7.5 centimetres) longer than the car enabled Moffat to reclaim a world record that had been taken from him by a Chinese stunt driver. He bested his rival by half a centimetre.

Back on the Farm

http://y2u.be/Jfop02mQcqQ

"At a couple of stages some bicycles went past me," Irish farmer Patrick Shalvey told the BBC. "That was a wee bit disconcerting." Nevertheless, Patrick successfully reversed his 30-year-old tractor and its trailer along the winding roads of County Cavan in Ireland to take the world record. Patrick also said he was cheered by the horn beeps of passing lorries, although, given the tail-back, you have to wonder whether they were all being supportive. Even with a police escort, it took him 2½ hours to travel the record 13 miles (21 kilometres).

▼ Ramping It Up

http://y2u.be/XUIiffRMfVQ

Ever wondered what skateboarders do for thrills when they grow out of their baggy shorts and elbow pads? Professional skateboarder Rob Dyrdek set 21 different skateboarding records before moving on to be a TV star and all-round entertainer. He broke doughnut-and-banana-eating records on his hit show *Rob & Big*, but once a ramp man ... In the parking lot of a theme park, Dyrdek reversed his Chevrolet Sonic off one ramp and flew 89 feet 3¼ inches (27.2 metres) through the air to land cleanly on another. What a guy!

THE WORLD'S LONGEST REVERSE RAMP JUMP

▶ Bowling Backwards

http://y2u.be/ex5iwpBHhdw

YouTube has opened up an opportunity for records to be broken all over the world. You no longer need officials and men in blazers to set an authentic record, just a clear video of your achievement. Step forward the most unlikely looking hero in Andrew Cowen of Illinois, USA. Andrew was determined to throw a 300 score (pretty impossible for us weekend bowlers) – while facing the wrong way. He managed 280 – two more than the official record – and might have reached his 300 if not for that second frame slip-up.

TOTALLY GROSS!

Are you ready to be completely grossed-out? These are some of the yuckiest, flesh-creeping and nauseating clips on the site. And, of course, they are absolutely mesmerizing.

Pardon Me

http://y2u.be/gU3jBonhsrQ

"The goal of the WBF, based in Geneva, is to restore burping to a place of respectability in Western culture and to remove the stigma that has attached itself to this practice during the past millennium." This is how, between hearty belches, a World Burping Federation spokesperson introduced the inaugural World Burping Championships at New York's Hudson Station Bar. This video features the competition's winner, Tim Janus, who set a world record with his 18.1-second-long burp. While happy with his prize, Tim seems eager for burping to become multi-discipline, setting his sights on future records in decibel burping and burp-talking.

MILK-SQUIRTING CHAMPION

▶ Squirt Off

http://y2u.be/H7EPl1N_aN4

It's the ultimate squirting-milk-from-the-eye battle! Please don't try this at home. It hurts and can lead to lasting damage to the eyes. Plus, it's altogether a pretty repulsive thing to do. That said, have a look at these two heroes squirting it out for the record. The trick, apparently, is to snort milk up your nose, close your mouth, block your nostrils and build up the pressure in the nose. The milk has nowhere else to go but to escape through a duct in the eyes. Yuk!

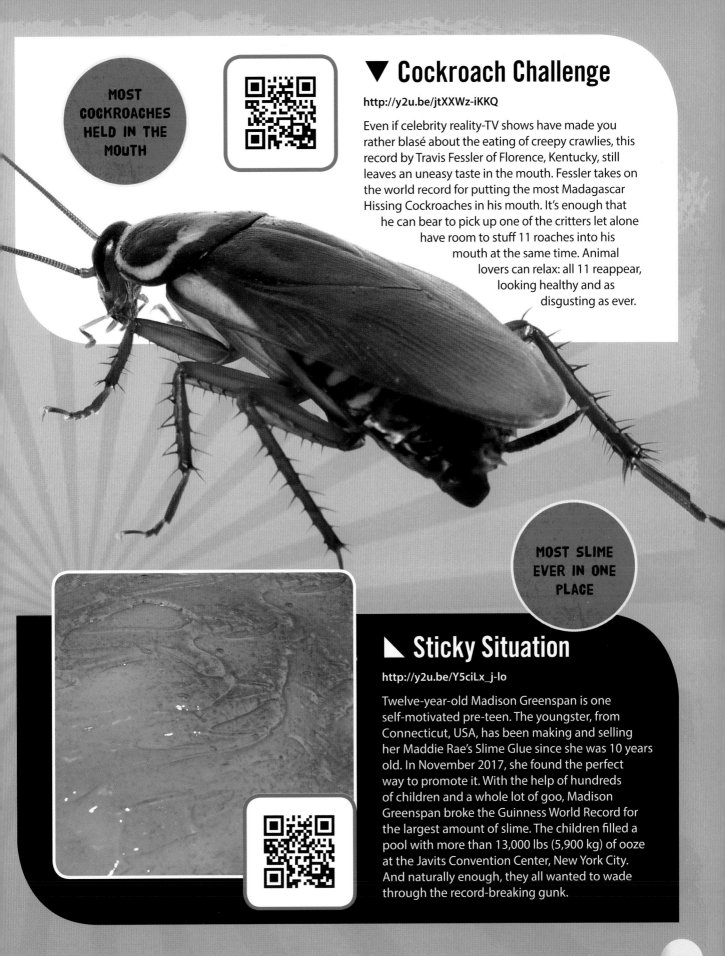

▼ Cockroach Challenge

http://y2u.be/jtXXWz-iKKQ

Even if celebrity reality-TV shows have made you rather blasé about the eating of creepy crawlies, this record by Travis Fessler of Florence, Kentucky, still leaves an uneasy taste in the mouth. Fessler takes on the world record for putting the most Madagascar Hissing Cockroaches in his mouth. It's enough that he can bear to pick up one of the critters let alone have room to stuff 11 roaches into his mouth at the same time. Animal lovers can relax: all 11 reappear, looking healthy and as disgusting as ever.

MOST SLIME EVER IN ONE PLACE

◣ Sticky Situation

http://y2u.be/Y5ciLx_j-lo

Twelve-year-old Madison Greenspan is one self-motivated pre-teen. The youngster, from Connecticut, USA, has been making and selling her Maddie Rae's Slime Glue since she was 10 years old. In November 2017, she found the perfect way to promote it. With the help of hundreds of children and a whole lot of goo, Madison Greenspan broke the Guinness World Record for the largest amount of slime. The children filled a pool with more than 13,000 lbs (5,900 kg) of ooze at the Javits Convention Center, New York City. And naturally enough, they all wanted to wade through the record-breaking gunk.

MULTIPLE RECORD HOLDERS

For some people, breaking one mention in the record books is just not enough. One sniff of glory has them searching for more.

JOE ALEXANDER

Pleased as Punch

http://y2u.be/yWeu2isK57U

Eighth-Dan black-belt Taekwondo Grand Master Jayanth Reddy is a whirling dervish, breaking records left, right, up and down with his lightning-fast fists and feet. Jayanth might have been in his forties when he notched up his first record, but he now holds 15 Guinness World Records, including breaking 34 cement blocks with spinning cartwheel kicks in a minute, executing 171 double roundhouse kicks in the same time and the most number of kicks (52) to remove an object from a height of six feet (1.82 metres). Most recently, he performed 352 jabs in a minute to become the world's fastest puncher.

◀ Joe of all Trades

http://y2u.be/vilul1gCm64

Joe Alexander from Hamburg, Germany, likes a record or two. Well, 10 at the last count. Joe doesn't seem fussy as long as they are records. Among his successes are smashing concrete tiles while holding an egg in his hand, catching marshmallows with chopsticks, and trapping harpoons underwater. On record-breaking day 2013, the self-styled Adrenalin Master gave us two records for the price of one. First up, he walked across 60 champagne bottles in a row without touching the ground. He then followed that up by catching 16 darts with his bare hands.

MOST MARSH-MALLOWS CAUGHT WITH CHOPSTICKS

🢂 Mr Olympic

http://y2u.be/OK0k6i2d_jk

"This all started with one little dream as a kid to change the sport of swimming and try to do something nobody has ever done," said US swimmer Michael Phelps. Well, he can tick that one off his to-do list. A gold in the men's 4x100 metres medley relay at the 2016 Rio Olympics took Michael Phelps's medal tally to 28 (23 gold, 3 silver and 2 bronze) – 10 more than the next most decorated Olympian, gymnast Larisa Latynina. Despite the announcement of his retirement after the Rio Games, many believe he could be back for more in 2020.

POP'S MOST SUCCESSFUL MUSICIAN

▲ Houston, We Have a ... Beatle

http://y2u.be/hpvE8kVGeZl

Once a member of the Beatles, Paul McCartney has gone on to become the most successful musician and composer in popular music history. He has a host of sales and radio-play world records, the most Number 1 hits ever, the most frequently covered song in history ('Yesterday' has been sung by over 4,000 artists), the largest paid audience for a solo concert (350,000 people, in 1989 in Brazil) – and, perhaps best of all, he was the first artist to broadcast live to space.

BRILLIANT BUILDINGS

Yes, it's interesting to discover the dates and dimensions of the world's record-breaking buildings, but how much better is it to watch one tilting sideways, or being climbed without ropes?

Head for Heights

http://y2u.be/a2p4BOGXSBw

Do you suffer from vertigo? If so, maybe give this video a miss. Here, a man known only as "Urban Endeavors" takes us up 1,500 feet (475 metres), twice the height of the Eiffel Tower, to the very top of the world's tallest TV tower, in North Dakota, USA. The tower itself is an unexceptional structure, but the journey is nail-biting and breathtaking as our guide climbs without ropes or harness; just gloves and bucketfuls of courage. He even forgoes the "easy way up", climbing the outside of the tower, rather than using the central ladder.

▶ Mesmerizing Moscow

http://y2u.be/FS17yy1rIsw

October 2015 saw the Moscow International "Circle of Light" Festival screen the world's largest projected image, a dazzling 205,582.33 feet^2 (19,099.3 metres^2) video animation, onto the iconic architecture of the Ministry of Defence building in Russia. Thousands of people turned up to become mesmerized by the vivid and vibrant visuals, a display that used 140 powerful Panasonic projectors to illuminate the 50-minute film in HD for all to see. Check it out!

LARGEST PROJECTED IMAGE

▶ A Tilt at the Record

http://y2u.be/UEfeqgXPHPA

Everyone has heard of the Leaning Tower of Pisa, some have heard of the leaning tower of Suurhusen (which leans a further 1.22 degrees). However, as of 2010, there is a new leaning king on the block – the Capital Gate in Abu Dhabi. In contrast to the previous record holders, the Capital Gate was intentionally designed to lean. Despite being one of the tallest buildings in the city at 35 storeys high, it keels as much as 18° westwards – more than four times that of Suurhusen.

▶ Plastic Fantastic

http://y2u.be/aVCxqiuDL7s

It has been called a movable, breathable, environmental miracle. It could be the first building constructed from garbage, but EcoARK is certainly the largest structure ever made from plastic bottles. The nine-storey deconstructable building in Taiwan was built for the 2010 Taipei International Expo. It is 426.5 feet (130 metres) long and is made from 1.52 million recycled PET bottles. The bricks are a 3D honeycomb of interlocking bottles, which makes it 50 per cent lighter than a conventional building, but it's tough enough to withstand 1.5 times the force of the worst hurricane recorded without any damage.

LARGEST BUILDING MADE FROM PLASTIC BOTTLES

King of the Castle

http://y2u.be/Qoqx24oXcoI

There's no sea and nowhere to lay a towel, but the landlocked German city of Duisburg does have a sandcastle – the biggest sandcastle ever made! Having failed in 2016 after a major castle collapse, the city succeeded the year after with a sandcastle that took 19 sculptors 3 weeks to build and used 4,000 metric tonnes of sand. Their 54.72-foot (16.68-metre) tower, built in a disused coal and steel plant, featured replicas of the Great Sphinx of Giza, Venice's Rialto Bridge, the graveside of Elvis Presley and other global landmarks.

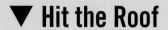

▼ Hit the Roof

http://y2u.be/iD4qsWnjsNU

The Khalifa Tower (Burj Khalifa), a skyscraper in Dubai, is the highest man-made structure in the world. Unsurprisingly, it has been a target for BASE jumpers wanting to set records. Two jumpers created a world record in 2008 when they illegally jumped from the 160th floor, but this 2014 "official" jump surpassed that. Fred Fugen and Vince Reffet leaped from a platform built above the top of the building, some 2,716 feet 6 inches (828 metres) from the ground. They actually did it six times to make sure the video was impressive!

THE
WORLD'S
TALLEST
BUILDING

SUPER-FAST RECORDS

The best records are those feats we think we can do pretty well ourselves. Just watch these people get dressed, cut hair or throw a Frisbee – and see if you might match them.

Dressed/Undressed

http://y2u.be/ksymwAItE0M

This one is just a bit of fun. Who would think it was possible to undress in less than a second? The speedy disrober is a Japanese actor and comedian called Herachonpe. His appearance on a Japanese TV show is a feature of many YouTube compilations as he has a unique way of taking his clothes off. It's got to be a world record, surely, and at the very least, it will raise a smile.

In the Balance

http://y2u.be/bDFZok9uzdk

Try to balance an egg. It isn't easy, they are just not made for it. It would take most people five minutes to balance one egg. Back in 2003, Brian Spotts helped break the record of most eggs balanced at once with 1,290 eggs. But he was hungry for more records, so he invented the category of fastest time to balance a dozen eggs. Finding his record broken, Brian decided it was time to poach it back – at a shopping mall in Hong Kong.

▼ Plot Twist

http://y2u.be/5x8jgGX3iNM

The Rubik's Cube was invented in 1974 (by Ernő Rubik, of course!) and first went on sale in 1980. With around 350 million cubes sold to date, it is the world's best-selling puzzle game. And a constant world-record challenge. Step forward SeungBeom Cho, the most recent record-breaker. He set his incredible 4.59-second record for the 3 x 3 x 3 cube in a competition in Chicago, USA in 2017. Now, 23-year-old Cho is a highly rated speed-cuber, but his surprise at taking the record is absolutely priceless.

FASTEST RUBIK'S CUBE SOLVER

▶ A Cut Above

http://y2u.be/C1k1kiAd3Bg

There was no time for niceties. No enquiry about holiday destinations. Not even a question about "how would you like your hair today, sir?" Hairdresser Konstantinos Koutoupis from Athens, Greece, had no time to waste if he was going to secure the record for giving the fastest haircut. The rules stated it had to be a "businessman haircut", taking at least half an inch (1.5 centimetres) off all round the head, so Konstantinos couldn't cut corners. With his mirrors cleaned, scissors sharpened and the customer's hair finely combed, Konstantinos had just 50 seconds to deliver…

▼ Sling Shot

http://y2u.be/NRr2zL0PYPA

You wouldn't want to get in the way of a 100-mph (160-km/h) ball thrown by an MLB baseball pitcher or, indeed, face a test cricketer bowling at you at 90 mph (145 km/h). It is, however, Jai Alai – popular in the Basque region, Latin America and the Philippines – that is recognised as the fastest sport in the world. Played on a 175-foot (53-metre) long court with three walls by teams of two players, each with curved baskets that are strapped to their hands, the game sees players consistently catch and throw balls at an incredible 186 mph (300 k/ph).

Speedy Frisbee

http://y2u.be/TO2RQj-L7gg

Simon Lizotte was a Frisbee prodigy. Dubbed "The Wunderkind", Lizotte, from Bremen in Germany, has dominated the German Disc Golf scene for years. He was the 2012 European Champion and is renowned in the game for his power on the drive. He holds the record for the longest disc throw (863.5 feet or 263.2 metres – the length of two-and-a-half football pitches), but here he notches up the fastest throw ever recorded at 89.5 mph (144 km/h).

WORLD'S
FASTEST
SPORT

SOUND AND VISION

They say it takes all sorts to make a world ... but the record world has the strangest inhabitants of all. Call them weird, call them mad; they call themselves "record breakers"!

Passing the Baton

http://y2u.be/hdflAVImhoU

"There are some difficult parts where the music gets faster, so I have to move my arms more, but I'm getting the hang of it." That's what Matthew Smith told *ITV News* in March 2017 during the Nottingham Symphony Orchestra's rehearsal for Johann Strauss's famous operetta *Die Fledermaus*. However, Matthew knew the piece by heart and, despite it being his first outing with the baton, he was confident of keeping the 75-strong orchestra on track. Which is all pretty impressive when you consider that Matthew is just 11 years old and the youngest ever symphony-orchestra conductor.

YOUNGEST SYMPHONY CONDUCTOR

▶ Korean Tweet

http://y2u.be/tNtcYIo6N04

K-Pop (Korean Pop) seems unstoppable in its conquest of the pop charts, and Seoul-based, seven-member boy band BTS are leading the way. BTS – also known as Bangtan Sonyeondan ("Bulletproof Boy Scouts" in Korean), Bangtan Boys or Beyond The Scene – were the first Korean artists to break the Top 10 on the US Billboard pop charts. Moreover, they rule social media. They have over 10 million fans on Twitter and, after the group's performance on the American Music Awards, they broke the record for the most Twitter engagements, their average 252,231 retweets and 634,246 likes per post surging past pop rival Harry Styles.

Press Record

http://y2u.be/xPGK84Yuihc

Vinyl records are hip again and to celebrate Jack White, formerly of The White Stripes, recorded a live version of his song "Lazeretto" and a cover of Elvis Presley's "Power of My Love". While he carried on entertaining the crowd, the masters were rushed off to be pressed and outfitted with sleeves featuring photos from the event. In just under four hours, the single was being bought in stores. Of course, he could have uploaded the songs to YouTube in a matter of moments, but that would have been far too easy!

MOST EXPENSIVE STAGE SHOW EVER

▲ Take the Stage

http://y2u.be/V1U-T_m3kMU

Irish rock band U2 like records – and not just the musical kind. Their 360° Tour in 2009–10 was not only the highest-grossing tour in history, but it also featured the largest stage and the loudest sound system. In other words, it was the most expensive show ever staged. On each of their 110 dates, Bono and the band played inside a huge arachnid – a 200-ton structure nicknamed "The Claw" – augmented by a million-piece video wall that needed 300 people to assemble. This fascinating time-lapse film captures it all as the super-size stage is put up and taken down again.

CRAZY CRITTERS

There's no such thing as a fair fight in the wild. Clawing, biting, stinging and kicking are all allowed. These guys are the best in the business.

Angry Bird

http://y2u.be/6Vqs2ZOOirk

Hailing from the rain forests of Australia and New Guinea, the cassowary has a bony crest on its head capable of knocking down small trees, and dagger-like sharp claws. Growing up to 6 feet (1.82 metres) tall and weighing in at over 130 pounds (59 kilograms), it can reach speeds of 30 mph (48 km/h) – and is capable of kicking with both legs at the same time. They have gutted dogs, slaughtered horses and maimed and even killed humans. The most dangerous bird by far …

Sting in the Tail

http://y2u.be/xb-0999E6qE

Say hello to the *Androctonus australis* – but don't get too close. The creature's name means "southern man-killer" and, indeed, the fat-tailed scorpion, as it is commonly known, is the deadliest scorpion in the world. Found in the deserts of the Middle East and Africa, the venom of the fat-tailed scorpion causes several human deaths every year. The killer critters aren't huge – they only grow up to 4 inches (10 centimetres) long – but are often found hiding in the brickwork or concrete cracks of houses. So go careful where you put those fingers!

▶ Packing a Punch

http://y2u.be/ti2Uoc1RXuQ

The mantis shrimp is a fabulous creature. A shrimp-sized lobster, it has big bug eyes, comes in dazzling colours and packs the fastest and strongest punch in the animal kingdom. Sometimes referred to as "thumb splitters", their claws are strong enough to split human appendages, and the shrimp has a punch stronger than a .22-calibre pistol. It has even been known to smash the glass of aquariums when riled. Just watch this slow-motion footage of this champion slugger throwing a right hook!

THE SHRIMP THAT PACKS A PUNCH

68

▶ Iron Jaws

http://y2u.be/akbpHX0Wbvw

The human bite exerts a pressure of around 120 psi (pounds per square inch). It's enough to chomp through an apple or a piece of toffee. Lions and sharks have jaws that are five times as strong – good for tearing raw flesh apart or ripping through a small boat. But the iron jaws of the animal world belong to the Nile crocodile. These beasts can snap at 2,500 psi (and have reached 6,000 psi), twice as much again as the feared shark.

▼ Highly Poisonous

http://y2u.be/UETfZLsWWAM

The inland taipan – or the fierce snake, as it is sometimes known – is the most poisonous snake on the planet. It lives in the dry areas of Australia and feeds on small mammals, its venom being especially adapted to kill them effectively. It is an extremely fast and agile snake, which can strike with extreme accuracy and almost always releases venom. One drop of its poison can kill around 100 full-grown men in as little as 30–45 minutes if left untreated.

THE WORLD'S MOST DEADLY SNAKE

AMAZING FOOD RECORDS

Groceries – they're not just for eating, you know. You can use them in art, construction, as a pastime – and to break records. Here's some food for thought ...

▶ Pumpkin Pride

http://y2u.be/8eQljtg3tAA

This was the moment the pumpkin world had been waiting for: the first-ever one-ton pumpkin, winning farmer Ron Wallace a $10,000 prize. The historical event happened in 2012 at the All New England Giant Pumpkin Weigh-Off when Wallace's colossal pumpkin was lifted onto the scale by a forklift truck. It topped out at an astounding 2,009 pounds (911 kilograms), beating the record set just the previous day by 165 pounds (75 kilograms) to become the largest fruit ever grown.

Absolutely Ridiculous, Seriously

http://y2u.be/L4Y6VVdk2XY

If the quarter-pounder at your local burger bar is a little insubstantial for you, take a trip to Mallie's Sports Grill & Bar in Detroit, USA. They pride themselves on their "Absolutely Ridiculous Burger", which breaks – and re-breaks – the world record for the largest hamburger commercially available. You'll need to give the restaurant 72 hours' notice and have $2,000 dollars to spare for the 165-pound (75-kilogram) burger. It takes 22 hours to cook and is served with 15 pounds (7 kilograms) of lettuce, 30 pounds (14 kilograms) of bacon, the same amount of tomatoes, and 36 pounds (16 kilograms) of cheese, all on a 50-pound bun (23-kilogram) bun.

THE INCREDIBLE ONE-TON PUMPKIN

◄ Coffee Break

http://y2u.be/Kng_LuXl6HI

Albanian artist Saimir Strati's previous work includes mosaic portraits of Leonardo Da Vinci with nails, a galloping horse with toothpicks and singer Michael Jackson with paint brushes. This time he made another mosaic – the largest in the world – with a million coffee beans. Strati says he wants his image of a Brazilian dancer, a Japanese drummer, an American country music singer, a European accordionist and an African drummer to spread the message of: "One world, one family, over a cup of coffee."

▼ Spaghetti Junction

http://y2u.be/v7SgBUq6_qk

Spaghetti Bridge competitions are held in universities around the world as a test for students' knowledge of engineering, physics and design. The bridges are made of only spaghetti and glue and are tested for how much weight they can sustain before they shatter. The Budapest Technical University has a great reputation for setting records and it was their students Miklós Vincze and Csaba Jaró who created Hoverla 5. A beautiful and, as it proved, historic construction, it finally collapsed under a weight of 1,257 pounds (570.3 kilograms).

RECORD-BREAKING SPAGHETTI

SUPER-STRENGTH RECORDS

The human body is a wonderful thing and even if you think you've seen it all, there's always something weird out there that will blow your mind: these record-breakers, for example.

On the Nail

http://y2u.be/W13JvvsKiJM

Extreme-stunts performer "Space Cowboy" calls himself "Australia's most prolific record breaker" – and with good reason. He has over 40 records to his name (which is really Chayne Hultgren), including pulling 411 kilograms by fishhooks in his eye sockets for the furthest distance, the fastest arrow caught blindfolded, and most chainsaw-juggling catches on a unicycle. In 2012, the Cowboy displayed his skills on the TV Show *Australia's Got Talent*. Lying on a bed of over 100 sharp, 8-inch (20-centimetre) nails, he was driven over by 20 motorcycles in 2 minutes.

◀ Busting his Nuts

http://y2u.be/OD1g8fUFdxQ

If you're struggling with the nutcracker again this Christmas, you could try breaking those shells manually. All you need is a little iron-palm training. That's how this martial-arts master gained the strength to set a new world record in Foshan City in southern China's Guangdong Province in 2017. He smashed 302 walnuts in 55 seconds with his bare hands. Before you give it a go, though, bear in mind that kung-fu expert Li Weijun has trained in various kinds of Chinese martial arts for over 27 years.

MONSTER WALNUT-CRUSHER

▶ A Nose-Blowing Champ

http://y2u.be/6LGiq717r9Q

23-year-old Jemal Tkeshelashvili is capable of inflating hot-water bottles to the point of bursting – with his nose! These rubber bottles require ten times more air pressure to inflate than a party balloon, so Jemal needs great lung capacity and the ability to push the air out of his nostrils with incredible force. Here, in 2009, in his home town of Tblisi, Georgia, he blew up and exploded three hot-water bottles in 23 seconds, including one being sat on by a hefty adult.

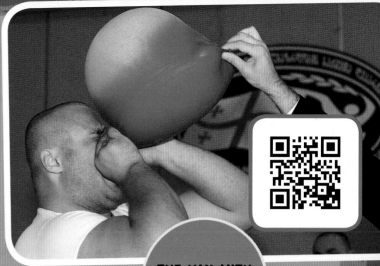

THE MAN WITH A CHAMPION NOSE

Thigh High

http://y2u.be/TN59gYxa2to

The sport of crushing fruit between your thighs isn't likely to threaten the popularity of football on TV any time soon, but Olga Liaschuk's appearance on British TV show *This Morning* caused quite a stir. Seated on a mat in the studio, and watched over by genial show hosts Phillip Schofield and Holly Willoughby, Olga crushed 3 watermelons between her thighs in just 14 seconds. Ukrainian Olga is also a champion in the perfectly respectable sport of weightlifting, but who wants to watch that when you can see exploding melons?

▼ Game of Throwing

http://y2u.be/MdcnUdzab7E

"I'd be a bloody fool if he didn't frighten me. He's freakish big and freakish strong and quicker than you'd expect for a man of that size." So says Bronn in the smash TV series *Game of Thrones* of the character played by impressive record breaker Hafþór Júlíus Björnsson. "The Mountain", as the 6-foot 6-inches (2-metres) tall, 405-pound (184-kilogram) giant is known in the TV series, also goes under the moniker Thor when he's competing in the World's Strongest Man competition. So, finally, we come to his record: a pretty impressive feat of throwing a 33-pound (15-kilogram) keg over 23 feet (7 metres) in the air.

Table Manners

http://y2u.be/MC6tgknKPQE

Even among strongmen challenges, some records push the boundaries of the bizarre. Take Georges Christen, a national hero in Luxembourg. In a career spanning over 30 years, Georges has made a name for himself setting records pulling trucks, buses and ships, and even making a huge Ferris wheel turn – all using his teeth. This performance – a repeat of another record-breaking feat – is a little more special. It shows a woman sitting on a table being carried in the air by Georges – yep, you've guessed it – in his teeth! She's seems like a willing participant, but keep an eye on her expression.

73

HOLDING OUT FOR A HERO

This awesome selection illustrates just how wide-ranging the record-breaking heroes are. Some rely on physical endurance, others on know-how and some are just downright crazy!

◀ Room on the Back

http://y2u.be/6qRzC95YpSE

Plumber Colin Furze's project began in his mum's garden with a normal 125cc scooter, which the ingenious engineer adapted with a home-made aluminium frame, adding 25 seats and extending it to 72 feet (22 metres) – nearly as long as a tennis court. To set the record, Furze had to ride the bike for 328 feet (100 metres), but he actually rode it for over a mile (1.6 kilometres). "When I first got on it, I thought it would never work, and at a slow speed it's almost impossible to keep upright," says Colin, but on Saltby Airfield in Grantham, England, he managed a pretty impressive 35 mph (56 km/h).

MOST DRUMBEATS IN A MINUTE

▶ Drumroll Please!

http://y2u.be/fsR_yDeYyGo

At the age of two and a half, Siddharth Nagarajan played his first concert and was officially recognized as the youngest ever Indian drummer. Six years later, having been invited onto a National Geographic TV show, he was declared an inborn genius. Now, at the age of 19, Siddharth is a respected percussionist across musical genres and a world-record holder. In 2017 he broke the record for The Most Drumbeats in a Minute Using Drumsticks. His 2,109 beats is equivalent to a staggering 35 beats in a second. Now that's how you "beat" a record.

▼ Fast Track

http://y2u.be/H7IwEQGM_Vk

There are many records in this book that are foolish, dangerous or outright idiotic, but this is the only one that is actually criminal. The clip tells the story of Ed Bolian's attempt at the Cannonball Baker Sea to Shining Sea Memorial Trophy Dash, a coast-to-coast drive across the USA and the basis for the movie *The Cannonball Run*. It's a highly illegal race that requires speed limits to be broken all through the journey. Ed reached a top speed of 158.26 mph (255 km/h) and spent 88 per cent of the trip above 80 mph (128 km/h), but he did traverse the country in just 28 hours and 50 minutes.

THE FASTEST DRIVE ACROSS THE USA

A High Rate of Inflation

http://y2u.be/u5B-dwMby74

Balloon artists are fun, knotting together balloons to make a dog, a flower or… well, usually a dog. Dave Baker has other ideas. He delights in creating "twisted wonderlands" from balloons. In 2015, Dave spent three months planning his record-breaking 16-foot (4.88-metre) high and 71-foot (22-metre) long vampire bat balloon sculpture. Inflating nearly 4,000 balloons, he carefully assembled the giant, upside-down-hanging bat. The impressively spooky installation was ready for Halloween.

THE BIGGEST BALLOON ANIMAL EVER

How Low Can You Go

http://y2u.be/AaPtiFO-NLc

Tim Storms goes deep for his record. He's no diver, though, as singer Tim holds the world record for reaching the lowest note. Due to his oversized vocal chords, Tim can hit notes so low that only huge animals like elephants can hear them. He has reached a G-7 or 0.189Hz – a note eight octaves below the lowest G on the piano (a whole piano length lower). This gives him another record – the greatest vocal range. He has a full 12 octaves, but Tim has warned he could break records again as his voice continues to get lower as he ages.

TOTALLY DIFFERENT

The record breaker can never stop to ask why. Thankfully, these record setters never questioned putting themselves in harm's way, playing a silly instrument or throwing shaving-foam pies …

Comfort Blanket

http://y2u.be/qK7RYDGj_xk

In February 2016, Mother India's Crochet Queens in Chennai, India, made the largest crochet blanket in the world. How big is it? It's massive! Measuring 120,001 feet² (11,148.5 metres²), the blanket covered an entire football pitch! Creating such a snuggly object took more than 1,000 participants (aged eight to 85), from more than 14 countries, scores of hours to create individual 40 x 40 inch (101.6 x 101.6 centimetres) sections, which were then sewn together to make one ultra-cosy blanket. After the record was verified, the blanket was deconstructed and the sections were donated to local charities.

WORLD'S LARGEST CROCHET BLANKET

▼ Splat's the way to do it!

http://y2u.be/sKOqUJfcUfw

And you think flinging foam pies is just clowns playing around? Listen, there are rules to this sport. The plates must be filled with shaving foam, which has to have a peak, and the flinger must be five feet (1.5 metres) away from the victim. And so to the Kidtropolis show in London in 2017, where "Captain Calamity" and "Colonel Custard" (probably not their real names) are on their fourth attempt at the record for the most shaving-foam pies flung in someone's face in one minute. They have already equalled the record but, if they are going to better it, they need to keep their eyes on the pies…

MOST "PIES" THROWN IN FACE

76

◀ Raw Geometry

http://y2u.be/C7XY-HvNWas

In the summer of 2016, sushi mosaics were trending on Instagram. Hundreds of pictures showed sushi squares, artistically arranged in colourful geometric patterns. It is a quintessentially Japanese art form – they are exquisite, delicate and precise – so, naturally, the world record for the largest sushi mosaic was set in… Norway, and was created by a chef who runs a sushi bar in Sweden. The mosaic, displayed at the Aspmyra Stadion, in Bode, Norway, measured an incredible 608 square feet (56.50 square metres) and included almost 1,800 pounds (800 kilograms) of salmon, around 900 pounds (400 kilograms) of rice, 44 gallons (200 litres) of rice vinegar, 1,060 pounds (480 kilograms) of cucumber and 22 pounds (10 kilograms) of chives.

WORLD'S LARGEST SUSHI MOSAIC

▶ Take a Bow – or Two

http://y2u.be/mPni3__sWus

Perhaps no one pointed out to Ukrainian musician Oleksandr Bozhyk that when a piece of music says it is a concerto for four violins, that does not mean they all have to be played by the same person. At a live concert in Lviv, Ukraine, in 2012, the virtuoso violinist took up two bows and four violins and proceeded to play – pretty well considering – the soundtrack from the film *Requiem for a Dream*. It was, of course, the most violins ever played by one person at the same time.

THE MOST VIOLINS IN ONE GO

COOL CAT RECORDS

There is plenty of kitten action and a lot of celebrity cats on YouTube, but not many make the record books. Here's a select few who are on the road to purr-fection.

Cat Concern

THE WORLD'S TALLEST CAT

http://y2u.be/d6In17HHz60

In November 2017, a fire swept through a house in Detroit. It was home to Arcturus, who held the record for the world's tallest domestic cat at 19 inches (48 centimetres) tall, and Cygnus, the cat with the world's longest tail – it stretched to 17 inches (43 centimetres). When the fire started, owners Will and Lauren Powers escaped, leaving the doors open to allow Arcturus, Cygnus and their other cats to flee. However, despite the offer of a $25,000 reward, the cats are still missing. Let's hope they're safe somewhere.

Fluffy Jumper

http://y2u.be/66pMRSIgIe0

Alley, a stray cat, was adopted after she was found looking frail and nervous in a city side street. Taken in by Chicago-based Samantha Martin, Alley had really landed on her feet, for Samantha is a trainer for the travelling cat circus Acro-cats (search for their videos on YouTube – they're really fun), and she quickly discovered that Alley loved to bounce around the platforms she used to teach her cats to jump. As Samantha began to train her, it became apparent that Alley had a real aptitude for jumping, leaping over 6 feet (1.8 metres). Could this street cat really become record-breaking royalty?

▶ Cool Cat

http://y2u.be/eCG-wlnJJK0

Cats are well known for having great balance. It's pretty useful for traversing garden fences or catching birds. Boomer, however, is far too cool for that kind of nonsense. The Bengali cat hangs out in Australia and likes nothing better than riding his skateboard. Here is Boomer, in October 2017, breaking his own record (13 people) for the longest human tunnel travelled through by a skateboarding cat. He propels himself through 20 pairs of legs – and still acts like it's really no big deal. He's obviously saving the high fives for his first 360 flip.

MOST TALENTED SKATE-BOARDING CAT

▶ Fat Cat

http://y2u.be/7dVn7KNP0co

Garfield is one of the great cartoon cats, right up there with Tom, Top Cat and Sylvester. Now, there is a real-life Garfield, who shared some of his animated namesake's gargantuan appetite and indolence. Garfield was brought to an animal rescue in Long Island, New York, after his owner passed away, and he shocked the volunteers with his obesity. He tipped the scales at 40 pounds (18 kilograms) – an average cat weighs around 10 pounds (4.5 kilograms) – and earned the distinction of being the fattest cat in the world.

THE WORLD'S FATTEST CAT

◢ Big Big Cat

http://y2u.be/xBznm54nVMM

There are cats, big cats and then there are ligers. Ligers are the offspring of a male lion and a tigress – huge animals that do not exist in the wild and are only bred in captivity. Hercules, who usually lives at the Myrtle Beach Safari wildlife preserve in South Carolina, is the biggest of them all. He is 6 feet (1.82 metres) tall, 12 feet (3.65 metres) long and weighs 900 pounds (408 kilograms) – as big as his parents combined. He may look a handful, but his keepers say he's a real pussycat.

THE WORLD'S LARGEST LIGER

79

CRAZY CROWD RECORDS

Whoever said "Three's a crowd" wasn't in the record-breaking business. To register in the record books, you need great organization, silly costumes and people in their thousands ...

▼ Who You Gonna Call?

http://y2u.be/dqQCj7WKNgk

"Ghostbusters of the world, gear up!" went the call to arms from Paul Feig, director of the 2016 version of the 1984 supernatural horror-comedy classic. The fans responded and 263 people got their ghost on – dressed up as the film's famous "no-ghost" logo – and gathered at Singapore's Marina Bay Sands to celebrate the launch of the all-female reboot of the *Ghostbusters* film. Star of the movie Melissa McCarthy was also in attendance and in high spirits as the assembly claimed the title of "Largest gathering of people dressed as ghosts at a single venue".

Follow the Leader

http://y2u.be/yg17h5H9YUM

The record for the most people singing in a round was previously held by the Dublin Google office, where 3,798 employees sang Pharell William's "Happy". The new record could not be more different, as to achieve it a choir of 4,166 people in Turkmenistan sang a song penned by the president. The performance of "Forward Only Forward, My Dear Country Turkmenistan" featured a big-screen video of President Berdimuhamedow himself playing a synthesizer and singing along with his people. The song was performed inside a giant yurt measuring 115 feet (35m) in height and 230 feet (70m) in diameter. Not exactly "Happy", but a record is a record.

WORLD'S LARGEST GHOST GATHERING

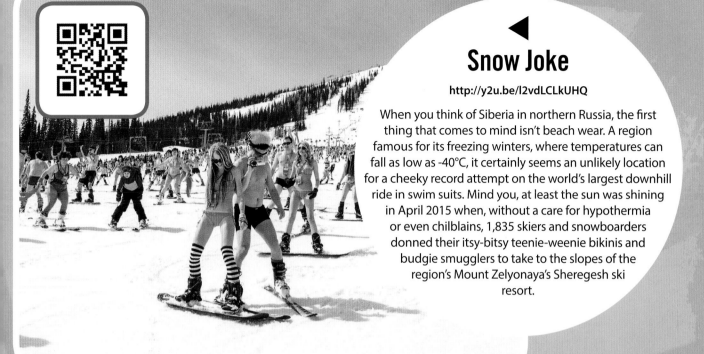

Snow Joke

http://y2u.be/l2vdLCLkUHQ

When you think of Siberia in northern Russia, the first thing that comes to mind isn't beach wear. A region famous for its freezing winters, where temperatures can fall as low as -40°C, it certainly seems an unlikely location for a cheeky record attempt on the world's largest downhill ride in swim suits. Mind you, at least the sun was shining in April 2015 when, without a care for hypothermia or even chilblains, 1,835 skiers and snowboarders donned their itsy-bitsy teenie-weenie bikinis and budgie smugglers to take to the slopes of the region's Mount Zelyonaya's Sheregesh ski resort.

▶ Flying the Flag

http://y2u.be/43tJndsYH3Q

India's rivalry with Pakistan is often hostile but, in December 2014, the stakes were raised when India stole the world record for the largest human flag from their neighbours. Over 50,000 volunteers began gathering at 5.00am in the YMCA ground in Chennai, but it wasn't until noon that they were in position to form the tri-colour flag. Pakistan's previous record was just short of 29,000 – they've probably already started working on recapturing the title.

▼ Ever So Elfish

http://y2u.be/lu8dsjoW5-o

Nearly two thousand Santa's little helpers, aged between nine and 15, put on red, green and white hats, matching T-shirts and pointy plastic elf ears, and formed up outside a shopping mall in Bangkok. Those participating were required to stand still for 10 minutes with their elf ears and hats on. Some didn't make it and others were disqualified for not putting on their elf ears, but 1,792 correctly attired and standing still were enough to set a new record.

RECORD-BREAKING NUMBER OF ELVES

RECORD-BREAKING DOGS

It's dog beat dog in the competition for canine records. You'll love these proud pooches as they show off their record-breaking skills.

THE UGLIEST DOG IN THE WORLD

◀ Ugly Mutt

http://y2u.be/7AkYSGllKTk

Two-year-old Peanut, a mutt who is suspected of being a Chihuahua/Shitzu mix, doesn't have a lot going for him. He was seriously burned as a puppy and lived in an animal shelter for nine months before he found a home. On the looks side, he has matted hair, protruding teeth and looks as much rodent as canine. However, Peanut found fame in California in 2014. In a hotly contested competition, he swept the floor with the other hideous hounds and was crowned the World's Ugliest Dog.

Bursting with Joy

http://y2u.be/j00meODyF-g

If there was ever a dog Olympics, the balloon-popping event would surely be up there with toy hiding and squirrel chasing. Setting about a room full of balloons with paws, claws and teeth has athleticism, skill, excitement and is absolutely hilarious. Here's the current record owner showing how it's done. Californian Jack Russell terrier Twinkie, whose mother, Anastacia, held the title for 7 years until 2015, focuses hard and pops 100 balloons in just 39.08 seconds. That's two and a half balloons per second – no wonder she looks pleased with herself. Give that dog a biscuit!

BIGGEST DOG IN THE WORLD

Got this Licked

http://y2u.be/-jsMpxIXaTY

Mochi, or 'Mo' to his friends, is an adorable eight-year-old St Bernard from Sioux Falls, South Dakota. While many dogs like a good slobber, Mo has an advantage – he officially has the longest tongue (on a dog) in the world, with his licker measuring a whopping 7.31 inches (18.58 centimetres). That makes Mo rather good at both licking his own face and cleaning out the peanut-butter jar. Although his owner does have a job mopping up the excessive slobber, she can't help but admit that his loveable personality and charm make it all worthwhile.

▲ Dog Has His Day

http://y2u.be/29NPJDf2qto

As the runt of the litter, nobody expected Freddy to reach any great height. Now five years old, the Great Dane has been crowned the tallest dog in the world. This big, friendly giant measures 41 inches (104.14 centimetres) from his paws to his shoulders, and stands 7 feet and 6 inches (2.29 metres) when on his hind legs. A resident of Leigh-on-Sea in Essex, UK, Freddy is one hungry hound and scoffs down 1 kilogram of minced beef, 250 grams of steak and about 300 grams of liver every day, although he also has a penchant for chicken, peanut butter – and sofas!

THE WORLD'S SMALLEST DOG

▲ Pocket-Sized Pooch

http://y2u.be/fTEIdAyYkac

Like many dogs, Heaven Sent Brandy, the Chihuahua from Florida, USA, is not allowed on the furniture. In her case, it's just because if she jumps off, she'd break a bone. Measuring just 6 inches (15.2 centimetres) from tail to nose, the adorable four-year-old is no bigger than a can of cola and is the world's smallest dog in terms of length. She's a nervous little creature – but who can blame her, when every hulking great human in sight wants to cuddle her?

ENDURING PASSION

Breaking records can require years of grooming, hundreds of hours of practice, meticulous arrangement or serious organization skills. And some just happen in an instance of pure chance.

▶ The Uber

http://y2u.be/YR6Wh2Zy9jE

Uber driver Anthony struck lucky – or possibly unlucky – when he picked up Jimmy Donaldson in North Carolina. For Jimmy Donaldson is also Mr Beast, a YouTuber famous for such jinks as counting to 100,000 and tipping pizza-delivery guys $10,000. Mr Beast was looking for a ride to California on the west coast – a mere 2,256 miles (3,630 kilometres) away. Once Anthony had checked with his wife and called in sick at work, the longest Uber trip ever was on – and it was going to cost a beastly $5,500.

LONGEST UBER JOURNEY EVER

▼ Heavy Metal

http://y2u.be/5UrG-hY8kUc

Frenchman Michel Lotito is honoured with having the strangest recorded diet and it is fair to say that he didn't earn the nickname "Monsieur Mangetout" without tucking into a few odd items. As a child, Lotito suffered from pica, a compulsive disorder in which people eat non-food items. Developing his affliction into an act, he went on to devour beds, television sets, bicycles and shopping carts. His *pièce de résistance* was a Cessna 150 airplane, which took him two years to consume. Lotito died of natural causes in 2007, having partaken of almost nine tons of metal in his lifetime.

▶ Never Too Old

http://y2u.be/iD7D8BY2d1c

You're never too old to start exercising. That's what we can learn from athlete Charles Eugster, the 200-metre indoor-dash record holder – in the 95-years-and-over category. The former dentist was born in London in 1919 and, having started rowing at 63 and taken up bodybuilding at the age of 87, running was a natural progression for him, even though he was 95 before he took to the track. A self-confessed "hopeless runner" in his younger days, after a short training period, Eugster was soon outshining the elite in his age category. His time, by the way, was 55.48 seconds.

FASTEST VIOLINIST IN THE WORLD

▲ On the Fiddle

http://y2u.be/PA_1oS8Ch4U

Record holder Ben Lee is no novelty violinist. He was a child prodigy; a student at the London School of Music; played with the Arctic Monkeys, McFly and others; and eventually formed successful rock violin duo Fuse. In the summer of 2009, Lee suffered damage to his right hand and wrist after being run over by a truck while cycling. To inspire his rehabilitation, his bandmate challenged him to break the world record for fastest violinist. In fact, he went on to break the record five times, on both acoustic and electric violin.

Get Stuck In

http://y2u.be/ZAA3GFdKbCM

The idea for a world-record sticker ball came on the first ever National Sticker Day (who knew?), on 13 January 2016. Saul – for the ball has a name – sits in the reception of Sticker Giant, a custom-sticker supplier in Colorado, USA. When he set the record for biggest-ever sticker ball, Saul was made up of 171,466 stickers, which measured 9 feet (2.75 metres) around and weighed in at 231.6 lbs (105 kg). After running for president in 2016 (don't ask) under the motto "Stick together", Saul has apparently put on weight – every visitor adds a sticker to his girth.

AMAZING ATHLETES

Every sport has its record breakers. These stars, whether from well-known sports like football and swimming, or less well-known, like balloon-batting, have some amazing achievements to crow about!

Surface Tension

http://y2u.be/DIACWkiBO2Q

The world record for the 50-metre backstroke stands at 24.04 seconds, but an American, Hill Taylor, can claim to have swum it a whole second faster than that. The time set by the Texan-born phenomenon known as "Dolphin Man" was ignored as he swam the whole lap without taking a single stroke. As the swimmers rise on 15 metres (as stated in the rules) to begin their classic backstrokes, Hill Taylor never surfaces, preferring to swim underwater. Demolishing the field, he surges ahead using a combination of a unique streamlined position and an amazingly powerful dolphin kick.

▼ Up in the Air

http://y2u.be/dOzzQmMsN2Q

"I know it's silly and kind of dumb, but... I'm pretty proud of myself." This video is like a seven-minute version of *Rocky* – a story of determination, hard work and following your dream. Buzzfeed employees Liem, Katelyn and Jeremy had a chance to write their names in the history books by keeping three balloons in the air for a minimum of 5 minutes and 35 seconds. Easy? Apparently not, but Jeremy is not one to give up easily. Surely, with a little training, he can break that record! This is his story. And good fun it is too.

BEST BALLOON BATTERS

► Lucky Punt

http://y2u.be/2j_sMqTx240

Seeing a goalkeeper score is one of football's great collector's items. When the ball was passed back from the kick-off to English team Stoke City's Bosnia and Herzegovina international goalkeeper Asmir Begovic, his intention wasn't to join the small band of keeper-scorers. However, with just 13 seconds left on the clock, his up-field punt caught the wind and bounced over opposite number Artur Boruc into the Southampton team's net. It was the sixth-fastest goal in Premier League history but, more importantly, at 301 feet (91.9 metres), it was the longest in competitive football anywhere in the world.

▼ Jump at the Chance

http://y2u.be/kPZvtlDLjpl

This is an unofficial world record, but there appears no reason to doubt it – and it is exceptional. It features Kevin Bania, a CrossFit athlete (CrossFit is a sport featuring weightlifting, sprinting and jumping exercises). Bania attempts a record standing box jump, which involves jumping onto a box or level surface. From a standing start, he leaps from the floor to a platform 5 feet 4.5 inches (1.63 metres) high. Bania himself stands 5 feet 10 inches (1.78 metres) tall, so he is within six inches (15 centimetres) of jumping his own height.

THE MAN WHO JUMPS ALMOST AS HIGH AS HIMSELF

WILD SPORTS

Terrified by the high board at the pool? Dizzy on the top storey of the multi-storey car park? Then perhaps you should just sit down and watch some people who know no fear ...

▼ New Ball Game

http://y2u.be/NehU-6NCBco

Zorbing is the sport of rolling down a hill in the kind of plastic sphere given to bored hamsters. Protected by a pocket of air between them and the edges of the ball, the participants can thrust the ball forward but have limited control over the direction. Miguel Ferrero from Spain, nicknamed "The Adventurer", was encased in a Zorb ball and threw himself down a ski run at La Molina in the Pyrenees. He reached a record speed of 31.2mph (50.2km/h).

THE FASTEST ZORBING ON RECORD

◄ Extreme Swimming

http://y2u.be/IJY8VgmvXHc

Diana Nyad became the first person to swim the 100 miles (160 kilometres) from Cuba to Florida without a protective shark cage. Braving rough seas, the fear of shark attack, vomiting from salt-water intake and wearing a heavy suit to withstand jellyfish stings, Diana succeeded on her fifth attempt over 35 years – her fourth since turning 60.

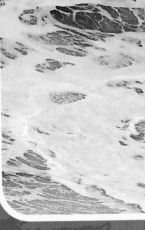

Snow Business

http://y2u.be/f0mTTmOuvUQ

France's Edmond Plawczyk had waited a long time to reclaim his snowboarding speed record. He had originally set the world record in 1997, but that was broken in 1999. April 2015 was payback time as Edmond donned his strange-looking red winged suit and aerodynamic helmet at the top of the slopes of the famous Chabrières piste in the French Alps. He was soon flying down the 4,600-foot (1,400-metre) course, which at one point measured a gradient of 98 per cent, to realise his ambition and a new record speed of 126.309 mph (203.275 km/h). Sweet.

▼ Surf's Up and Up

http://y2u.be/74pnrYPozcU

Surfing legend Garrett McNamara caught a towering 100-foot (30.5-metre) wave off the coast of Nazare in Portugal. Risking being slammed into a reef or the ocean floor, he beat his own record by 1 foot (30 centimetres). That too was set off Nazare, where an underwater canyon generates some of the world's biggest waves. "You are just going so fast," McNamara told ABC Television. "And you're just chattering, flying down this bumpy, bumpy mountain. Your brain is getting rattled. Your whole body is getting rattled."

THE LARGEST WAVE EVER SURFED

TRULY REMARKABLE

It's a wonderful record-breaking world and YouTube contributors across the globe are out filming every remarkable event and achievement.

Suds and Scrubs

http://y2u.be/b4zLZB4cPBU

In a state whose unofficial motto is "Go Big or Go Home!", Buc-ee's Car Wash in the town of Katy has stepped up to the plate. Buc-ee's were a chain of convenience stores known for Beaver Nuggets, Texas-themed tourist trinkets and immaculate bathrooms, but now they have a new boast. The Katy store has the longest car-wash conveyor belt. Measuring 255 feet (77.72 metres) long with 25 foam brushes and 17 blowers, it takes 5 minutes for a dirty car to enter at one end and emerge clean at the exit.

▼ Pop-Up Painting

http://y2u.be/RwtWZd-sbMc

In June 2014, world-famous Chinese artist Yang Yongchun unveiled a special piece of art. Named *Rhythms of Youth*, it depicted the impressive architectural landscape of Nanjing and the Yangtze River that runs through it. Not only was it the largest and longest street painting in the world, measuring an astonishing 1,200 feet (365 metres) long and covering 28,000 sq. feet (2,600 sq. metres), but it was also an anamorphic painting – created in a distorted manner to make it appear three-dimensional.

THE LONGEST STREET PAINTING

▶ A Fine Line

http://y2u.be/y4VJssQv_Qw

Domino-line topples – you either love them or you hate them. If you fall into the latter category, best move along. For the rest of us, there is something hypnotic and satisfying about dominoes falling one by one. This is a single line, so no effects, no dominoes lifted by cranes or toppled by balls – just straightforward domino action. And, after spending two days putting 15,524 multi-coloured dominoes in line and initiating a 5-minute toppling sequence, professional domino artist Lily Hevesh earned the record for the longest domino line ever. Exquisite.

LONGEST LINE OF DOMINOES EVER TOPPLED

▼ Water Colours

http://y2u.be/RfEPdy3NNlo

Jesper Kikkenborg is a Danish marine biologist and artist. Combining both his fields of expertise, he produced a painting at the Blue Planet Aquarium in Denmark. This was no ordinary painting, though: Kikkenborg wore scuba-diving gear and painted his picture inside the 4-million-litre Ocean Tank. Named *Mother of the Sea*, it featured eagle rays, hammerhead sharks and other exotic fish. It took him 23 hours over nine days and measures 48 sq. feet (4.5 sq. metres) – the largest underwater painting ever.

A Real Blast

http://y2u.be/5Oeiiqv XBkw

The best firework displays always keep something special back for the grand finale of the show. The display for the Feast of St Catherine in Zurrieq, Malta, certainly didn't disappoint. The crowds that had gathered at one of the island's biggest festivals witnessed the spectacle of the world's single biggest firework. The rocket, called the *ballun tal-blalen* (which loosely translates as "balloon of balls"), exploded from a 10-foot-wide (3-metre) shell weighing 570 pounds (260 kilograms), launching a chain reaction that saw the whole sky covered in chrysanthemum-pattern lights. Enjoy – it may not last long, but the brief effect is completely dazzling.

THE
HIGHEST-
EVER LEGO
TOWER

▼ Tower Power

http://y2u.be/KuQkUmz9fmY

They might make film heroes now but, for years, Lego bricks were purely for construction. Thankfully, some are still preserving the art of the interlocking brick. In the shadow of St Stephen's Basilica in Budapest, children, locals and Danish engineers constructed the highest-ever Lego tower. Rising 114 feet (34.76 metres), the towering spire was made of 450,000 colourful bricks and appropriately topped with another great toy – the Rubik's Cube, a puzzle designed by a Hungarian professor of architecture, Ernő Rubik.

IT TAKES ALL SORTS

Isn't it a wonderful record-breaking world when a twerking champion and an underwear-wearer can share a page with the world's greatest footballing cyclist?

▼ Hard Twerk

http://y2u.be/otZmEyIDGsY

After Miley Cyrus's twerking at the 2013 MTV Video Music Awards, New Orleans rapper Big Freedia set about reclaiming the dance. The self-proclaimed Queen of Bounce claimed twerking had been started by the "bounce" dance scene of New Orleans. So, in her home town, Big Freedia – the stage name of Freddie Ross – cued her hit "Duffy", and led a world record 410 dancers, ranging from age 8 to 80, as they shook their rumps for two continuous minutes.

CHAMPION TWERKING IN NEW ORLEANS

▼ Everybody Freeze!

http://y2u.be/BrfN_o91lgg

Autumn 2016 and a new craze was sweeping the Internet: the Mannequin Challenge. Across numerous platforms, people shared videos of groups acting as if they had been frozen in time. Perhaps the most famous video came from the White House and featured Bruce Springsteen, Tom Hanks, Diana Ross and others (you can view it on YouTube). Of course, competition for the biggest Mannequin Challenge was soon on, with pride of place going to this magnificent effort by 55,000 spectators, players, staff and paramedics at a Cape Town sevens rugby tournament in South Africa's Cape Town Stadium.

WORLD'S LARGEST MANNEQUIN CHALLENGE

On My Head!

http://y2u.be/joA086aXDlk

As a Nigerian footballer in Cambodia, the possibility existed that Harrison Chinedu might have got overlooked by the national team's coaches. But Harrison was hard to miss when, kitted out in the national strip, he rode a bicycle from a beach outside Nigeria's capital Lagos all the way into the city to the national stadium. Oh, did I forget to say that he did the whole 64 miles (103 kilometres) balancing a football on his head? Six months earlier, his record walk with a ball on his head (28.84 miles/48.04 kilometres) had been quickly broken, so this time he's hoping he's in the record books to stay.

That's Just Pants

http://y2u.be/ov0x6cjGX38

You want to break a record? It doesn't matter how bizarre it is, you need a plan. Take Silvio Sabba, a prolific record-breaker from Milan, Italy. Silvio is attempting to break the record for pulling on the maximum number of underpants in 30 seconds – he needs to wear 13 pairs. Firstly, Silvio is organised. He arranges the underpants on the table in the order he will put them on. Secondly, Silvio has clearly trained – 13 leaps and hitches in a short time will take its toll. Finally, and most importantly, he has perfected his technique – a two-footed jump that achieves both height and accuracy.

97

▼ Pulling Faces

http://y2u.be/Sp4M2GcnRlE

Tang Shuquan of Chengdu City, China, spends a lot of time hoping the wind doesn't change direction and he stays "like that". Named the King of Deformed Faces, Tang spent 10 years working on being able to contort his face into the ugliest shapes possible. After winning the world record for gurning, Tang, who has the extraordinary ability of biting his own nose, even challenged all-comers – offering a £10,000 prize to anyone who can match his face-stretching skills.

THE GURNING WORLD CHAMPION

MAD MOVIE RECORDS

Roll the credits! From Bollywood to Hollywood, the glamorous and exciting world of the movies lists the famous and the not so famous in its annals of achievement.

AN EXPENSIVE RECORD BREAKER

◀ Titanic Record

http://y2u.be/2e-eXJ6HgkQ

The 1997 film *Titanic* starring Leonardo DiCaprio and Kate Winslet was, at the time, the most expensive film ever made. It was worth it. *Titanic* became the most successful film ever in terms of box-office and critical success. It has the most Oscar nominations (14, tied with *All About Eve*) and the most Oscar Awards (11, tied with *Ben-Hur*) and is the second-highest-grossing film ever (*Avatar* is first), having taken over 2.2 billion dollars at the box office.

A Dress to Impress

http://y2u.be/RPW3kavkoFQ

On 19 May 1962, during the 45th-birthday celebrations for President John F. Kennedy, actress Marilyn Monroe sashayed onto the stage at Madison Square Garden, took off her fur coat and famously sang "Happy Birthday, Mr President". Under that fur coat Marilyn was wearing a sheer, sequinned dress so tight that she had to be sewed into it. It was an era-defining moment. Fast-forward 54 years and that same dress is under the hammer at auction. It was bought by Ripley's Believe It or Not for an incredible $4.8 million (£3.7 million), making it the most expensive dress ever.

THE WORLD'S TINIEST MOVIE EVER "FILMED"

▲ Minute Movie

http://y2u.be/oSCX78-8-q0

Like many great movies, *A Boy and His Atom* has a heart-warming friendship at its centre and – no spoilers here – a moving ending. It has been watched over 6 million times since it was uploaded in 2013, which is particularly astounding as it can't really be seen by the human eye. IBM researchers used a scanning, tunnelling microscope to move thousands of carbon-monoxide molecules (two atoms stacked on top of each other) to make a film so small it can be seen only when you magnify it 100 million times. It's the world's smallest stop-motion movie.

Extra Special

http://y2u.be/miuzO4yI0V4

Acclaimed director Richard Attenborough faced a real challenge when filming *Gandhi* on location in India in 1980. He was determined to re-create the great man's life as accurately as possible and had to film a funeral scene in which a million people had lined the route. Attenborough chose to film on the thirty-third anniversary of Gandhi's funeral and managed to recruit around 300,000 volunteers and actors – the most extras ever to appear in a feature film.

It's Been Emoji-nal!

http://y2u.be/HZcaMuR9yrE

Back in the 20th century, there was just the smiley. Now, 50 years on, that happy face has given birth to over a thousand emojis, which are used across messaging and social media. They even have their own day – 17 June is World Emoji Day. In 2017, to celebrate the release of the blockbuster film *The Emoji Movie*, Sony Pictures assembled emoji-dressed crowds in London, Dubai, Moscow, Dublin and Sao Paulo. Some 531 people dressed as the characters, including winking face, smiling face, pizza and poop emoji. It became the largest ever group of people dressed as emojis.

TRANSPORT RECORDS

This collection of the bizarre, brilliant, marvellous and downright silly means of transport would get some strange looks down the High Street.

Lawnmower Mover

http://y2u.be/nF18um9VGp8

Next time you complain about mowing your scrubby 10-foot (3-metre) patch of grass, consider investing in a Honda Mean Mower. With a custom-made Cobra sports seat, a six-speed gear system and a fibreglass cutter deck, Honda claims their machine is the world's fastest mower. It is capable of speeds of up to 130 mph (210 km/h). Piers Ward of the BBC's *Top Gear* magazine took the grass-cutting speedster for a burn-up in Tarragona, Spain, and managed 116.57 mph (187.60 km/h) – it was, indeed, a lawnmower land-speed record!

▼ All the Fun of the Fair

http://y2u.be/fGr0oifJMEI

Shouty Colin Furze (watch his fun videos) is a modern-day, record-breaking hero. He's the creator of the world's longest motorbike, the world's fastest pram, the world's fastest toilet and numerous other hilarious and impressive inventions and modifications. His latest project is the world's fastest fairground dodgem car, to be driven by the Stig from TV's *Top Gear* series. Adding a 600-cc Honda motorbike engine will help raise the dodgem's normal speed of 5 mph (8 km/h), but can it make the required 100 mph (160 km/h)? Just hope there's nothing coming in the opposite direction!

THE WORLD'S FASTEST DODGEM

One-Wheeled Wonder

http://y2u.be/Jzeq7FWl3Dg

The idea behind the monowheel is simple: build a big enough wheel and you can fit a person inside. Motorized monowheels have been around since the 1930s, but issues with balance, steering and visibility make them dangerous to ride. Kevin Scott built his monowheel, *War Horse*, from a 200cc go-kart engine. It has a diameter of 59 inches (1.5 metres) and the only way to change direction is by leaning. Nevertheless, in September 2016, in Yorkshire, England, Kev rode along an airstrip and back, clocking up a record speed of 61 mph (98.5 km/h).

◣ Time for Bed

http://y2u.be/CQYWX9UaCjQ

Tom Onslow-Cole is a top British racing driver who specializes in driving souped-up road cars and sports cars. His recent triumph, however, came in bed – a speeding bed. Tom travelled to the Emirates Motorplex dragstrip in the United Arab Emirates to drive a motorized bed, based on a specially modified Ford Mustang. Never one to be caught napping, he hit a top speed of 84 mph (135 km/h). Tom has held a world record before. In 2012, he helped drive the world's fastest milk float. In 2014, that record was broken, but at least he won't lose any sleep over it now.

WORLD'S HEAVIEST WORKING BICYCLE

▲ Heavy Going

http://y2u.be/Zm3ROyV1dhA

You won't see this kind of bike steaming up Alpe D'Huez in the Tour de France, but Frank Dose's extraordinary vehicle is already a winner. The bike, which took him six months to build, broke the record for the heaviest bike in the world, weighing in at over one ton. Despite the fact that it sports 5-foot (1.53-metre) diameter tyres from an industrial fertiliser spreader, a frame made from scrap steel and a beer-crate saddle, Frank still managed to pedal the required 328 feet (100 metres) to earn himself the record.

BIZARRE PEOPLE

The say: "If you've got it, flaunt it." None of these record breakers seems to have any problem flaunting their special features. And, as you will discover, they are pretty special ...

▼ Tongue-Tied

http://y2u.be/h3Ys5aWrbNc

Byron Schlenker always thought his tongue was a real mouthful but never dreamed it could be a record breaker until he helped his daughter, Emily, 14, with a school project. Seeing a picture of an Australian man who claimed to have the world's widest tongue, he began to wonder if his own tongue measured up. Soon he discovered that not only did he have an even wider tongue, but also that Emily had the record female equivalent! Byron's measures a whopping 3 ⅜ inches (8.6 centimetres) across – ¾ inch (2 centimetres) wider than an iPhone 6 – and Emily is not far behind at 2 ⅞ inches (7.3 centimetres).

LARGEST TONGUES IN THE WORLD

◀ The Eyes Have It

http://y2u.be/8n14AmSWbAg

The average person's eyelashes measure 1 centimetre (0.39 inches) or so. They do their job of protecting the eye pretty well. Some people apply alluring false eyelashes, which extend their length to around 1.5 centimetres (0.59 inches), but Shanghai-born You Jianxia has eyelashes that reach an incredible 12.4 centimetres (nearly five inches). They hang down the side of her eyes to her mouth like jungle vines or delicate school-gym climbing ropes. You claims her lashes only began to grow after she retired from her high-status finance post and started spending more time in her garden, and she credits the amazing length to being at one with nature.

▶ What a Waist

http://y2u.be/kiUMBIwFbik

Cathie Jung first wore a corset at her wedding in 1969. She and her husband liked the look and now she is the corset queen – wearing the constrictive garment 24 hours a day. Her devotion to corsetry has enabled Cathie to reduce her waist to a record-breaking 15 inches (38 centimetres) – about the size of a jar of mayonnaise. It is an achievement even more remarkable when you consider her bust and hips are a pretty average 39 inches (99 centimetres).

Back to Front Boy

http://y2u.be/63h81dNRwRs

It was at a Minecraft conference in 2015 that 14-year-old Maxwell Day revealed his unique skill. Having seen a photo of the record-holder for largest foot rotation, he was soon demonstrating that he could rotate his right foot 157 degrees and turn his left foot round by 143 degrees, easily breaking the previous record of 120 degrees. Maxwell, from Enfield in the UK, asserts that he feels no pain when rotating his feet and he is able to walk with them rotated (although not fast enough to claim that record – yet).

105

EXTREME EATING

The world of competitive eating is not for the faint-hearted or for those brought up not to shovel down their food. But it is pretty amazing ...

Cone Madness

http://y2u.be/RfRDA1Tbwko

WORLD'S LARGEST ICE CREAM CONE

Being surrounded by freezing-cold temperatures, as well as constant snow and ice, you'd think that Norwegians would be sick to their stomachs at the thought of eating chilly ice cream. But not so. Norway's popular ice cream company, Hennig-Olsen, scooped a Guinness World Records title in July 2015 after creating the world's tallest ice cream cone ever – a magnificent 10 foot 1 inch (3.08 metres) feat of deliciousness! Weighing a ton, literally, the cone contained 1,080 litres (237.5 gallons) of strawberry ice cream – enough for 10,800 people to have two scoops each – and had to be airlifted to the event by helicopter!

I Scream, You Scream...

https://youtu.be/EaHrWPkWtOU

There was no brain freeze for Miki Sudo when she attended the first ever World Ice Cream Eating Championship at the Indiana State Fair in Indianapolis in 2017. Miki scoffed down 16.5 pints (9.38 litres) of vanilla ice cream in just six minutes. That's equivalent to around 28 large tubs of frozen deliciousness. Miki, of course, has form for this kind of thing. She is currently the top-ranked female competitive eater in the US and holds the records for fastest time to eat 50 Creme Eggs (6 minutes, 15 seconds) and chugging a gallon of milk before sky diving (54.25 seconds).

▶ Sprout About It

http://y2u.be/7Jl8gf2V98U

For many people, Brussels sprouts represent the unacceptable side of Christmas dinner, left on the side when all else has been polished off. Not for Emma Dalton, though. The surprisingly slim 27-year-old competitive eater, who has stuffed back a 5,000-calorie burger in under 10 minutes, has worked her way through the world's biggest helping of sprouts. In one sitting lasting just over half an hour, she scoffed 325 of the mini cabbages – that's almost 7 pounds (3 kilograms) of festive veg. Mind you, not even Emma seems to actually like sprouts, as she coated them in mint sauce, gravy and ketchup to help wash them down.

WORLD RECORD BRUSSELS SPROUTS EATER

▶ Kobayashi — the Master Eater

http://y2u.be/P1GBf0ioYKI

Kobayashi (see page 37) is arguably the world's greatest competitive eater. He has been blowing away his rivals in competitions for 15 years. He has pigged down hot dogs, tacos, satay, noodles and even cow brains, all in world-record time. Here is the master in action on a TV show in 2012, in which he set the record for most Twinkies eaten in a minute. A Twinkie is a "Golden Sponge Cake with Creamy Filling". One is delightful. Two can be sickly. Kobayashi ate 14 ...

THE CHAMPION COMPETITIVE EATER

▼ Blowing Bubbles

http://y2u.be/alBUeRNOaIw

Champion bubble blower Chad Fell of Alabama blew a bubblegum bubble with a diameter of 20 inches (50.8 centimetres) that remained intact for a full five seconds. It was no fluke. Chad takes his skill seriously. He gets through two bags of Dubble Bubble a week in practice and knows his science. He drinks cold water to regulate the temperature in his mouth and chews for 15 minutes to cut down the sugar to aid elasticity before carefully adding air.

▼ Oh, Crumbs

http://y2u.be/OZMMSW4Ackk

Many of the records in this book are impossible for readers to try at home. They are either dangerous, expensive, require specific skills or are just too gross. So here's one you can have a go at yourself. All you need is a chocolate muffin and a camera. Watch the video, study the tactics of Kyle Thomas Moyer of Pennsylvania, USA, who set the record for the fastest time to eat a muffin without using your hands, and prepare your attempt. The target to beat is 28.18 seconds, and remember: no hands!

Egg-ceptional

http://y2u.be/uCgok8lmVoI

Not only does speed-eating heroine Sonya Thomas rank among the best in her field, she also has the best nicknames. She sometimes goes under the fantastic moniker "The Leader of the Four Horsemen of the Esophagus". More often she is known as "The Black Widow" in recognition of the eight-stone petite woman's ability to out-eat men four times her size. As well as the feat seen here, Sonya holds a number of other records, not least consuming nearly five pounds of fruitcake in 10 minutes.

▼ Furious — and Tearful

http://y2u.be/Jky1gDSw0AM

Furious Pete (real name Pete Czerwinski) is a major player in the competitive eating world. He holds six world records, including polishing off 17 bananas in two minutes, wolfing down 15 hamburgers in 10 minutes, guzzling a bottle of olive oil (25 fluid ounces/750 millilitres) in 60 seconds, and tucking away 17 jaffa cakes in 60 seconds. Pete confesses, however, that eating a whole onion in 43 seconds was the toughest of all. Watch his first failed attempt, and you'll see why.

MULTIPLE FOOD-EATING WORLD RECORD HOLDER

NICE MOVES!

These entertaining clips pay homage to the hot-footers who have danced themselves into a pirouetting, head-spinning, pole-leaping, tip-tapping, mascot jiving, record-breaking world.

Spinning Queen

http://y2u.be/_bT756ywafU

Since she was 10, Sophia Maria Lucia has been America's darling. The young ballerina appeared on hit TV shows such as *Dancing with the Stars*, *America's Got Talent* and *The Ellen DeGeneres Show*. The dance prodigy has her own dancewear line and even a book. There is no denying the girl has talent and now she has a new nickname: "The Spinning Queen". In this clip, filmed in 2013, Sophia performs an amazing world-record 55 consecutive pirouettes.

▼ Body Popping

http://y2u.be/yHzpcBuQlpM

Julia Gunthel goes by the stage name Zlata. A 27-year-old Russian living in Germany, she is also known as the Most Flexible Woman on Earth. Watching the way she twists and bends her body around, it is hard to imagine that Julia actually has a spine. Her balloon-bursting act just has to be seen to be believed. She manages to burst three balloons in 12 seconds, using the curve of her back as a press. That just can't be comfortable.

▶ Human Propeller

http://y2u.be/EZfVAxG2-h4

The headspin, a staple power move of breakdancing, is a routine where the dancer's body is rotated while standing on his head. Just watch the poise and strength of 23-year-old Aichi Ono of Japan as it seems he tries to screw his head into the ground. The Human Tornado, or Spinboy as he is also called, spins at a breakneck speed, racking up an incredible 142 rotations in a minute on a TV show in Japan.

RECORD-BREAKING NUMBER OF HEADSPINS

Limbo Queen

http://y2u.be/tqI4NKLhhvU

Shemika Charles is the world-famous Limbo Queen. Ever since setting fire to the Guinness World Record for limbo-ing a mere 8.5 inches (21.5 centimetres) from the floor live on TV in 2010, Ms Charles has travelled the world, showing off her unique talent. In June 2015, however, the Limbo Queen took her skills to a whole new low – and limboed *under a car!* The first world record of its kind and genuinely unbelievable!

In a Spin

http://y2u.be/_U827SJO3Qw

Kinderdijk is famous for its 18th-century windmills – and now for the classic breakdance move that shares the name. More than 70 b-boys from the Netherlands, Italy and France gathered in front of the town's iconic structures to spin on their back and shoulders – a precarious move in the middle of the waterway. Nevertheless, they succeeded in setting a new world record for the number of simultaneous windmills performed in 30 seconds.

THAT'S GOTTA HURT!

"Now that has got to hurt." Sometimes you feel as if you are about to experience the pain yourself as you watch these record breakers undergo self-torture. Of course you aren't. Still, "Ouch!"

Doing His Nut

http://y2u.be/mkgDDCMKXXc

Next Christmas, when you are wrestling with a pair of nutcrackers and a walnut that won't crack, think back to this clip. It is from the Punjab Youth Festival in Lahore, Pakistan, in 2014. Here, martial-arts expert Mohammad Rashid sets about cracking 155 walnuts in only a minute – using his head. This man is deadly with his own nut, leaving just a wake of broken shells as he heads around the table at breakneck speed.

▼ Push-up Star

http://y2u.be/PdlpfOPCj9I

Super-fit fitness fanatic Carlton Williams, a man with very little body fat, has broken his own world record for the most push-ups successfully completed in 60 minutes. The 50-year-old Welshman achieved 2,220 complete push-ups – lowering his body until a 90-degree angle was attained at the elbow *for every single one* – at a gym in Margaret River, Western Australia, in August 2015. "After a while you just get used to the pain," he admitted afterwards. Be honest… how many could *you* do in an hour?

▼ The Flame Game

http://y2u.be/cNuwX0hTFKU

When you take a spoonful of soup and realise slightly too late that it's still too hot for you, that soup is around 85°C. If you're unlucky, your tongue will be blistered for a day or two. Now consider Brad Byers, a man nicknamed the "Human Tool Box" (because he can insert tools through his nasal cavities, but that's another story). Brad trumps your hot soup by more than 20 times as he extinguishes a propane blow torch on his tongue. Incredibly, he's basically licking a 2,000°C flame – what on earth can his tongue be made of?

► A Real Buzz!

http://y2u.be/8rlX4APbHTY

You may have heard of bee "beards" but watch this video and you'll see it's more of a bee full-face helmet – there are bees covering his whole face, head and shoulders! Juan Carlos Noguez Ortiz is the hero of the hour. After hanging a tiny cage containing the queen bee from his chin, a colony of 100,000 worker bees is released, huddling around her and settling over the rest of his face. Incredibly, Juan sits it out for 61 minutes as a crowd at Yonge-Dundas Square in Toronto looks on in admiration and bemusement.

MOST TIME SPENT COVERED IN BEES

▲ Heavy Metal

http://y2u.be/Rj7vKStJmtA

A living confusion of tattoo and glistening metal, Elaine Davidson is the world's most-pierced woman. A Brazilian-born nurse, living in Edinburgh, Elaine has 462 studs and rings (192 on her face), which saw her crowned the world's most-pierced woman in 2000. But Elaine didn't stop there – as of March 2012, she had amassed over 9,000 piercings. She never removes the rings and studs, which means she carries around an extra 6.6 pounds (3 kilograms). But you wouldn't miss her in a crowd!

THE WOMAN WITH THE MOST PIERCINGS

THE MOST EXPENSIVE

You'll be surprised at some of the things that turn up in the "most expensive" basket in the YouTube supermarket. Who would expect some scorpion venom next to a masterpiece?

◀ Flight of Fancy

http://y2u.be/s2d_XiJHmdI

If you're taking a flight from New York City to Sydney, why not travel in style? In fact, why not book a flight on Etihad Airways' Airbus A380? Ask for their luxury suite, "The Residence". At a mere $52,000, it's the world's most expensive flight. The five-star suite comprises an elegantly furnished double bedroom, a lounge with a flat-screen TV and a shower room, and comes complete with a Savoy Hotel trained butler to prepare your bed and ensure your comfort. What's that? You're booked in economy? Oh well, maybe you can wangle an upgrade! This video shows the first lavish leg of the trip

▼ Top Dollar Masterpiece

http://y2u.be/IQF6QFEY4Ps

Salvator Mundi was suddenly the name on everyone's lips. No, he hadn't just scored a last-minute goal in the World Cup Final. *Salvator Mundi* ("Saviour of the World") was a 500-year-old painting of Christ believed to have been painted by Leonardo da Vinci. In 2017 it sold in New York for a record $450 million (£341 million). The painting, showing Christ with one hand raised, the other holding a glass sphere, sold at auction in 1958 for a mere £45, so was it the most important art discovery of the century or an overpriced gamble by rich investors?

THE MOST EXPENSIVE WORK OF ART

◀ Sting in the Tale

http://y2u.be/RCcY0n_7DDs

The list of the most expensive liquids on earth is fascinating: perfume, champagne and human blood are all predictably on the list; there are some surprises like maple syrup and nasal spray; and no computer user would be surprised to see printer ink near the top at around $8,000 a gallon. Just be thankful, then, that you don't need too much scorpion venom (used in anti-cancer drugs). Scorpions are difficult and dangerous to obtain and milk (see the video!) and their venom fetches an amazing $40 million a gallon.

Time is Money

http://y2u.be/1_QCxOkCQHw

Paul Newman, who died in 2008, was one of the Hollywood greats – a fantastic star of many 1960s and 1970s films. In 1968 his wife, Joanne Woodward, bought him a Rolex Cosmograph Daytona watch from a Tiffany & Co. store in New York and had it engraved with the message "Drive carefully" (Newman had recently taken up motor racing). The Oscar-winning actor wore the watch every day for 15 years and it became so synonymous with his style that the model was called the "Paul Newman watch". In 2017 it was put up for auction and, selling for $17.8 million (£13.5 million), became the most expensive wristwatch ever sold.

▲ It's Not About the Money

http://y2u.be/QsT9tDqBCB4

THE MOST-EXPENSIVE FOOTBALL PLAYER

'It isn't about the money,' insisted Brazilian soccer star Neymar Jr on joining Paris Saint Germain in August 2017. Journalists, however, spoke of little else when PSG activated his $263-million release clause from Barcelona – as the BBC commentator remarked, for that money they could have bought three Boeing 737-700 passenger planes or enough spaghetti to cover the whole of Barcelona. And, they weren't finished there. Neymar's five-year contract is reportedly worth around $45 million a year before tax, making him the highest-paid player in the history of the sport. Is he worth it? This clip shows why PSG had every reason to be pleased with their purchase…

A LONG WAY DOWN

Some people just have no respect for the laws of gravity. It might have kept sensible folk's feet on the ground for centuries, but not your adrenaline-junkie record breaker ...

The Birdman of Norway

http://y2u.be/ER1PGYe9UZA

Is it a bird? Is it a plane? No. It's Espen Fadnes, the World's Fastest-Flying Human Being. In his flying-squirrel suit, Norwegian Espen routinely leaps off buildings, bridges, mountains and cliffs – and flies. Winning a base-jumping competition in 2010, he officially became the fastest-flying human. Just watch as he calmly (although, to be fair, he admits he's completely terrified) steps off a 4,068-foot (1,240-metre) cliff in Stryn, Norway, and flies through the air at speeds of over 150 mph (250 km/h).

Jump de Triomphe

http://y2u.be/MLejkyXbJlc

Australian motorcycle stunt rider Robbie Maddison likes a New Year's Eve party; his record-breaking end-of-year stunts have become a tradition for the thrill-seeker. Few of them can beat the 2008 effort when the 27-year-old sped his bike off a 35-foot (10-metre) high ramp to the top of the 96-foot (30-metre) high replica of the Arc de Triomphe in Las Vegas. Having set the world record for the highest motorcycle jump, he then plunged the 80-foot (24-metre) drop back – breaking his hand in the process.

THE FASTEST BARE-HAND CLIMBER

▼ Look Mum, Just Hands!

http://y2u.be/Wy3SuhEQHVg

Dan Osman was the fastest bare-handed speed climber in the world. In this ascent, he climbs Bears Reach, a 400-foot (122-metre) rock face of Lover's Leap in California, in just 4 minutes, 25 seconds. He uses no ropes or grips, just gaining hold with his feet and his bare hands. Osman held other mountain-stunt world records, including a freefall rope jump of 1,100 feet (335 metres) at the Leaning Tower in Yosemite, California. Sadly, this was also the spot where he met his death after a tragic rope malfunction.

Skyfull

http://y2u.be/SJZ1b8-M4T4

The skies were alive in Arizona in 2017 as the Sequential Games welcomed sky divers from around the world. A few records were blown sky-high, but none more impressively than this mass dive in which 217 sky divers leaped simultaneously from 10 different aircrafts at an altitude of 19,000 feet (5,791 metres). Hurtling to the ground at a speed of 120 mph (193 km/h), they somehow came together from all across the sky, linking up in a giant snowflake-shaped pattern. Suddenly, they were changing positions, the view from above similar to a human kaleidoscope, to become the largest ever group to complete two and three different formations while free-falling.

THE LARGEST MASS SKY DIVE EVER

▲Walking the Walk

http://y2u.be/9W0umbacmzg

In China, Adili Wuxor is known as the "prince of tightrope walking", so his special skill won't be a surprise. The feat itself might impress, though. The 45-year-old Wuxor breaks his own record by walking a wire that's 5,905 feet (1,800 metres) long and about 590 feet (180 metres) above the ground across the Yellow River. He pauses at the centre for over half an hour, performing various stunts on the 1.5-inch-thick wire (3.6-centimetre) as he waits for his assistant, who started at the other end. He then proceeds to walk over him and continues his epic walk to the end of the wire.

COOL CONSTRUCTIONS

The world of engineering deserves a special mention in the record-breaking hall of fame. The world's greatest tunnels and bridges are spectacular examples of human achievement.

▶ Bridge of Size

http://y2u.be/WP1rZrB9SZI

Opened in 2009, the Sidu River Bridge in Hubei Province of China is the highest bridge in the world. It is a suspension bridge that hangs a vertiginous 1,600 feet (496 metres) above the river gorge. It spans just over 5,000 feet (1,5124 metres) across the river valley; far enough that builders had to use a rocket to string the first pilot line. Some claim it is also the only bridge in the world high enough for a person to reach terminal velocity if they were to jump off.

THE WORLD'S HIGHEST BRIDGE

◀ Cliff Hanger

http://y2u.be/HPs3Y6DMcY8

Can't be bothered to climb that mountain? No matter. Take the elevator instead. Well, you can if you take the Bailong Elevator at the Zhangjiajie National Forest Park in Hunan, China. The world's tallest outdoor lift, it also claims records for the world's tallest double-deck sightseeing elevator and the world's fastest passenger elevator with the biggest carrying capacity. It transports visitors to the top of a 1,070-foot (326-metre) cliff in less than two minutes. If you prefer to stroll up the valley, it will take you two and a half hours!

▲ Stairway to Heaven

http://y2u.be/T2HHh5ksUvI

High above the breathtaking scenery of China's Zhangjiajie National Forest Park is a white bridge, which seems to sit in the clouds. The Zhangjiajie Grand Canyon Glass Bridge is believed to be the world's longest and tallest glass pedestrian bridge. Located in an area that inspired the floating Hallelujah Mountains of James Cameron's movie *Avatar*, the 1,410-foot (430-metre) bridge stands nearly 984 feet (300 metres) above the ground. Glass panels set into its walkway give visitors vertigo-inducing views and photo opportunities of the canyon below. "It creates an experience of being in pure nature while suspended in mid-air," said the architect, Haim Dotan.

Little Big Town

http://y2u.be/O8TsKEtR8VQ

Welcome to Casey, Illinois, just a three-hour drive south of Chicago, USA. It might only have a population of 3,000 but this little town is onto a big thing. In 2011, local man Jim Bolin made a 56-foot (17-metre) wind chime to draw business to his wife's tea shop. He and other town folk then crafted a golf tee (29.5 feet/9 metres), wooden shoes (12 feet/3.6 metres wide), a pitchfork (60 feet/18 metres long), a rocking chair (55 feet/17 metres), a mailbox (33 feet/10 metres), and set of knitting needles (13 feet/4 metres) with crochet hook (6 feet/1.8 metres) – all world-record-sized!

THE MOST-DANGEROUS TUNNEL

◣ Cliffhanger

http://y2u.be/GzJnOrr5RUE

Located in the Taihang Mountains of China, the Guoliang Tunnel is deemed the World's Most Dangerous Tunnel. In 1972, inhabitants of the village of Guoliang dug a tunnel 3,937 feet (1,200 metres) long through the rocky cliff. When opened to traffic it was soon dubbed "the road that does not tolerate any mistakes". A tight squeeze for even one vehicle, it twists and turns past 30 or so "windows", which provide views off the precipice to a tumbling abyss hundreds of feet below.

WILD RECORD BREAKERS

Another scan of the great achievers of the wild world brings forth the slow-motion sloth, the aggressive ant, the super-sized sheep and a rather disgusting beetle.

THE WORLD'S SLOWEST ANIMAL

▼ Beware of the Bull

http://y2u.be/vU_thoOeQw0

The bulldog ant – also called a bull ant or jumper ant – is the hard case of the insect world. The World's Most Dangerous Ant, it is built for fighting. It measures a whopping 0.59–1.4 inches (15–36 millimetres) in length, has long mandibles and a venomous sting that inflicts death on other insects and great pain to larger creatures. But what gives them the edge is their fearlessness. They don't take kindly to visitors and will take on anything that comes near, even snakes and humans.

▲ Sloth Motion

http://y2u.be/OTp8W251aiQ

The three-toed sloth doesn't do anything in a hurry. It likes to sleep for around 10 hours a day, come down from its tree once a week to do its business and occasionally have a (slow) swim. These are the World's Slowest Mammals, averaging a distance of only 0.15 miles (0.24 kilometres) an hour, with a top speed of 6.5 feet (1.98 metres) a minute. They are so slow that algae grow on them. They do, however, have a good excuse; their long claws, ideal for tree life, make walking particularly uncomfortable.

▶ A Dung Deal

http://y2u.be/l1RHmSm36aE

Forget the gorilla or the rhino – the strongest creature on the planet rolls poo into balls and takes it home for supper. The dung beetle is the world's strongest insect and out-muscles every other animal. Dung beetles can pull 1,141 times their own body weight. This is the equivalent of an average person pulling six double-decker buses full of people. Their incredible strength is, of course, useful for pushing those balls of faeces, but also for pushing out rivals trying to enter their under-dung mating tunnels.

THE WORLD'S STRONGEST ANIMAL

◀ Woolly Sweater

http://y2u.be/kHu-r4gx2kI

Ramblers in Mulligans Flat Woodland Sanctuary outside Canberra, Australia, came across an extraordinary creature. It was the size of a small car and as woolly as a Yeti – it was Chris: a lost and very overgrown merino sheep. The world's woolliest sheep was in a bad way and, carrying five times his normal coat, it's doubtful if he would have survived the fierce heat of the Australian summer. However, shorn of almost half his body weight, Chris was found to be in surprisingly good health and he yielded 89 pounds (40 kilograms) of wool – the equivalent of 30 sweaters.

SPECTACULAR SCIENCE

Making new discoveries and inventions and exploring deeper and further than ever is the business of the scientist. So it is no surprise that they set some pretty incredible records.

Wonderstuff

http://y2u.be/WFacA6OwCjA

Graphene is a thin layer of pure carbon; it is a single, tightly packed layer of carbon atoms that are bonded together in a hexagonal honeycomb lattice. It is the thinnest, lightest and toughest material known to man, as well as being the best conductor of heat and electricity. Recent scientific breakthroughs in its production have led to predictions that it will soon be used in everything from bullet-proof clothing to fold-up televisions and phones, and even invisibility cloaks.

▼ Goodbye Moon

http://y2u.be/TU6QzMItdZA

Only 12 men have even taken a step on the Moon. Just three years after Neil Armstrong's first great step, Eugene Cernan prepared to climb back into *Apollo 17* as the last man on the Moon. While there, Cernan set the land speed record in the Lunar Rover, 11.2 mph (18.0 km/h), and spent a longer time than anyone else on the lunar surface. "When I pulled up the ladder," he said. "I knew I wasn't going to be coming this way again."

THE LuNAR SuRFACE LAND SPEED RECORD

▲ Do the Math!

http://y2u.be/aSg2Db3jF_4

The Mandelbrot set is a pretty complex mathematical concept that you can look up at your leisure – good luck with that! Mathematicians are still trying to solve some of its mysteries so, if you think you're going to get a simple explanation here, think again! In the meantime, have a look at this because it's awesome. The zooming in on an infinite process creates a mind-blowing set of swirling colourful images, rather like diving into an endless psychedelic pool. This is the record number of iterations, which makes this visual feast well worth including in this book.

▶ Leading Light

http://y2u.be/3bIXUBXj070

LIGHTEST SOLID MATERIAL IN THE WORLD

Clever Chinese scientists have created the world's lightest solid material – a graphene aerogel that is seven times lighter than air and 12 per cent lighter than the previous record holder. The sponge-like matter, made of freeze-dried carbon and graphene oxide, is also the thinnest material ever made – a pile of 3 million graphene sheets stands just 1/32 of an inch (1 millimetre) high – but its unique structure also makes it very light and strong. In fact, the claim is that a single sheet as thin as Clingfilm could withstand the weight of an elephant.

UNLIKELY CELEBRITIES

The millions of YouTube viewers can create the most unlikely celebrity record breakers. Among the surprising super-achievers are a scooting dog and a bunch of dancing hardened criminals.

▼ Exercise Yard

http://y2u.be/vsG1_eee9fg

The Philippines prisoners' dance to "Thriller" was a YouTube hit and is still worth viewing, but this full-body resistance workout by prison inmates in Peru broke their world record for the most people dancing in a prison. The colourful display was the result of three months' practice by around 1,200 prisoners at the overcrowded Lurigancho prison in Lima. The workout saw the prisoners – many of them murderers, drug barons and other serious offenders – strutting their stuff to the sounds of the beats of reggaeton and merengue.

MOST PRISONERS DANCING EVER

▲ Quick Hit

http://y2u.be/0E00Zuayv9Q

"I have a pen. I have an apple. Apple-pen! I have a pen. I have [a] pineapple. Pineapple-pen!" Oh, you mock now but, once you hear it, you'll be singing it all day long. The song "Pen-Pineapple-Apple-Pen" by Piko-Taro, a 40-year-old Japanese DJ, tapped perfectly into the winning formula of catchy lyrics, a memorable beat and a hilariously simple dance routine. His YouTube video has now garnered more than 100 million views, his Facebook video has had 70 million views, and his single – a mere 45 seconds in length – became the shortest song ever to make the Top 100 in the US.

Amazing Afro

http://y2u.be/65-He8_sb_k

Fourteen years ago, inspired by an old photo of her mother sporting an afro hairstyle, Aevin Dugas from Louisiana, USA, swapped her straight locks for her own natural round style. Now she sports the world's largest natural afro, measuring 4 feet 4 inches (1.32 metres) around and 7 inches (17cm) tall. It takes two days to wash and dry her afro and she sometimes struggles to see out from it, but she does admit it makes for a really comfortable pillow.

▼ Dog on Wheels

http://y2u.be/qKYryJ_1poQ

He's a three-year-old French sheepdog with a special talent. Ever since he was a puppy, Norman has been climbing on board a scooter and propelling himself along. Norman balances himself on the scooter with his two front paws on the handle and a back paw on the scooter. He uses his other hind paw to push himself forward. Having already earned the moniker "Norman the Scooter Dog", he then scooted 100 metres in just over 20 seconds – a world record for a dog on a scooter!

BEST CANINE ON A SCOOTER

A Real Mouthful

http://y2u.be/PampEBRmyzQ

Vijay Kumar of Bangalore, India, is getting used to the words "open wide". It's not just the dentist who wants to peer into the mouth of this world-record holder, for Vijay has 37 teeth in his mouth – five more than the average person and more than anyone else in the world. Vijay first noticed his bite was unusual as a teen, but only when he reached his 20s did he think of checking just how toothy he was. He does complain of biting his tongue but, on the other hand, he never has any trouble chewing toffee!

WORLD OF WONDER

Movie star George Clooney famously said, "I go on YouTube when somebody says to look something up." I wonder if he found any of these fabulous clips?

▼ You Know Who

http://y2u.be/EDQqEJWOUH4

In August 2017 a Welsh schoolgirl aged just 13 was named the world's biggest *Doctor Who* super-fan. Lily Connors fell in love with the timelord when she was just three years old. What began as a few second-hand action figures passed on by her father became an astonishing collection of 6,641 items of *Doctor Who* memorabilia. Through pocket-money purchases and gifts from family, friends and even *Doctor Who* actors, her collection includes figurines, sonic screwdrivers, posters and – in pride of place – a Tardis wardrobe made by her father and signed by the 12th Doctor, Peter Capaldi.

▲ Carpet World

http://y2u.be/JeEqpKr1vFg

Each year during the holy week preceding Easter, "sawdust carpets" line the city streets in Guatemala. Made of fine, brightly coloured sawdust with dried fruit, flowers and bread, they create an incredible street art of varying and often intricate design. In Guatemala City in April 2014, the longest-ever sawdust carpet was laid. Using an estimated 54 tons of dyed sawdust, it measured 6,600 feet (2,012 metres) long – but in days was trampled away by religious processions .

LARGEST DR WHO COLLECTION

▼ Security Blanket

http://y2u.be/vvNSqXN0E6g

Things are moving pretty fast in China these days. The two-lane concrete Zhuan-yang viaduct running through the town of Wuhan, in Hubei, central China had only been built in 1997. Just 16 years later it was deemed insufficient for the growing population of the city and, in order to replace it with a six-lane highway, the largest ever reinforced-concrete-bridge demolition was planned. However, with power cables and gas pipes laid alongside and thousands living by the road, engineers needed to tread carefully, smothering the blast under a huge blanket.

WORLD'S BIGGEST BLANKET

A Lot of Nerf

http://y2u.be/57MKxz4pJKE

"Nerf or Nothin' – Accept No Substitutes" runs the slogan for Hasbro's Nerf Blaster toy gun. This, however, is one substitute that's rather tempting. Former NASA engineer Mark Rober got together with YouTubers the Eclectical Engineers to construct the world's largest Nerf Gun. The shooter, which looks remarkably like the real thing, is around 5 feet (1.5 metres) long. Powered by a paintball air tank, it can shoot plastic darts at around 40 mph (64 km/h) from a distance of over 325 feet (100 metres). It might be a little bulky for a school bag, but you'd have no trouble from the class bully!

◀ Out of this World

http://y2u.be/E-mR4LCi9nk

A long time ago, in an era far, far away, a special movie spawned a whole array of related merchandising. In 1977, Steve Sansweet was working at the *Wall Street Journal* and came across a promotional book for an upcoming film called *Star Wars* – it began a lifetime obsession. The film generated a myriad of associated products and Steve began to collect them. Now housed in a 9,000-square-foot (850-square-metre) facility an hour north of San Francisco named Rancho Obi-Wan, his display – the biggest *Star Wars* collection in the world – numbers around 90,000 items with another 200,000 or so in storage awaiting classification.

▼ It's All Relative

http://y2u.be/WebTR66FJPc

Sect leader Ziona Chana has 39 wives – all sharing a 100-room mansion in a holy village in India. The largest family in the world lists 32 sons, 18 daughters, 22 grandsons, 26 granddaughters and seven great-grandchildren all living under one roof. While the youngest wife gets the bedroom next to Ziona, the eldest wife runs the household and organizes the meals, which can see them preparing 30 chickens, peeling 130 pounds (59 kilograms) of potatoes and boiling more than 200 pounds (91 kilograms) of rice.

THE LARGEST FAMILY IN THE WORLD

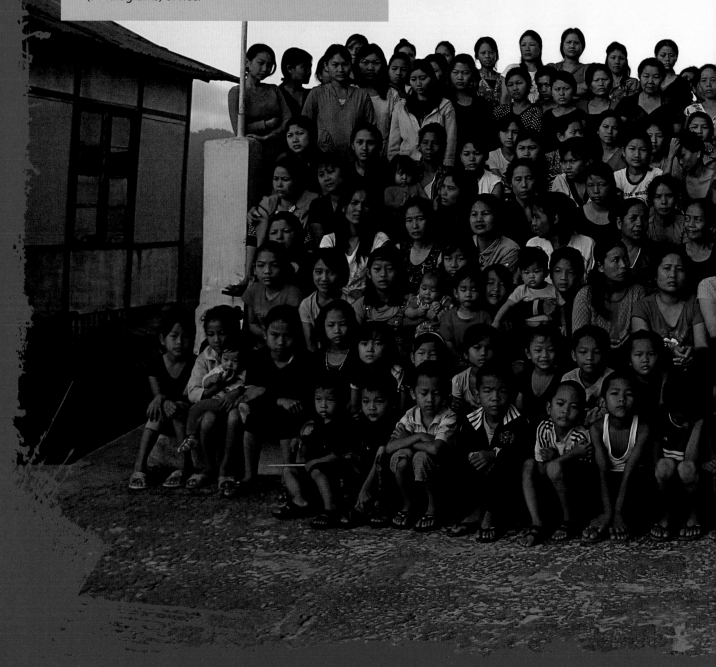

PEOPLE POWER

One day in the far-flung future, everyone will hold a record for something. These guys have already made their mark, but there's a record out there for everyone …

Off His Trolley

http://y2u.be/HcCoVFhdO3g

This crazy record-breaking invention is guaranteed to make the trip to the supermarket a lot more fun. Rodney Rucker of Arizona, USA, has created a shopping trolley 16 feet (4.8 metres) tall and V8-powered – the largest motorized shopping cart in the world. This fantastic vehicle sits six people comfortably in the basket, with another person behind the wheel in the "child's seat". The trolley can comfortably cruise along at 60 mph (96 km/h), but it's probably best not to do that down the frozen-vegetable aisle.

▼ Hard Core

http://y2u.be/pTeuBq1ai5g

They say an apple a day keeps the doctor away, but probably not the way Johnny Strange deals with them. The British daredevil, bored with breaking the record for the heaviest weight lifted by pierced ears (33 pounds/14.9 kilograms), looked for something even more impressive. So he took to chopping apples... with a chainsaw… while holding them in his mouth. Johnny claims he's never had any accidents, but that's not simply good fortune. He puts it down to meticulous practice, explaining that it normally takes about two years to bring a trick to the stage.

▶ It's a Twister

http://y2u.be/DwL993LKsFU

Most of us remember going head over heels. Tuck your head in and propel yourself forward. Well, Liu Teng, China's most flexible woman, does something similar – but almost back to front. The 24-year-old, often called the "Queen of Contortion", already held jaw-dropping records for an extreme back-bend off the edge of a table and using her foot to pick up a drinking glass, as well as for the fastest time to travel 65 feet (20 metres) in a contortion roll. In 2017 she broke her own record for the latter in a quite extraordinary and elegant movement.

▶ Heads Up, Bro!

http://y2u.be/Iq_HaPrRmJM

Fans of TV's *Game of Thrones* might recognise the setting for this record as the Great Sept of Baelor. It is, in fact, the Cathedral of Girona in Spain, where Vietnamese circus artists Giang Quoc Co and Giang Quoc Nghiep chose to perform their amazing world-record head-to-head balancing act. The acrobats climbed 90 of the picturesque steps of the cathedral in one minute with one brother balanced on top of the other, using only head-to-head contact. It wasn't the time for the brothers to fall out and, fortunately, they kept clear heads and held any sibling rivalry in check.

WORLD'S BEST BALANCERS

▶ High Kicking

http://y2u.be/sL4xS2t2Yk0

Twenty-three-year-old Canadian Silvana Shamuon is no novelty act. Silvana has been practising martial arts for over 17 years. She received her junior black belt at the age of 11, was inducted into the Universal Black Belt Hall of Fame in 2007 and represents her country in international tournaments. So, for a bit of fun, Silvana attempted the world record for the most items kicked off people's heads in one minute. Students from her old high school lined up wearing American football helmets fitted with kicking tees and footballs. Needing to beat 67 for the record, Silvana wound up her powerful kicking leg…

▼ Bearded Woman

http://y2u.be/rgQjfcpG7XY

After enduring years of bullying, 25-year-old Harnaam Kaur turned herself into a body-confidence advocate, model and Instagram star. The brave story of the youngest woman to have a full beard is an inspiring one. Diagnosed with polycystic ovaries, Harnaam has had facial hair since the age of 12. She suffered abuse and threats but, at the age of 15, decided to stop hiding and confront gender stereotypes. She never looked back. As she told the *Guardian* newspaper, "They can try to make a freak show out of me, but my voice and my message [are] much stronger than that. I have power in my voice."

RECORD-BREAKING ROBOTS

Science fiction doesn't seem to stay in the films and books for very long these days. Drones are everywhere, maybe keeping a close eye on the dancing robots in the record books.

Drone Delivery

http://y2u.be/vNySOrI2Ny8

In recent years, drones have been used for more and more every day functions. With technology becoming cheaper and drones stepping into our lives in almost every way, it was only a matter of time before Amazon sent their first *extra* special delivery. In December 2016, Amazon sent the very first drone package using Prime Air to Richard B. in Cambridge, England. Taking only 13 minutes to arrive from the moment it was ordered, this was an impressive display from the Internet giant. Richard B. looked pretty pleased with the service at least!

▼ Eye in the Sky

http://y2u.be/u-vxo_yMQwk

Up, down, left, right… No matter where you look these days, drones are never far away. They have become our eyes in the skies. In November 2015, Intel Corporation lit up the skies above the Flugplatz Ahrenlohe in Tornesch, near Hamburg, Germany, with 100 small drones flying in fantastic formation. A year later, in November 2016, they went one better – or 400 to be precise – with 500 drones all controlled by one pilot. Acting as one, they created a stunning Technicolor light show as dazzling as any fireworks display. It's unbelievable, and earned Intel a Guinness World Record for most unmanned aerial vehicles.

LARGEST DRONE DISPLAY

▼ Do the Robot

http://y2u.be/QfocjOJrm3c

Not happy just to take our jobs and drive our cars, robots are now threatening to make boy bands obsolete! Just watch these knee-high Dobi robots go as 1,069 of them set a record for the most robots dancing simultaneously. The nearly perfectly executed dance, which took place in Guangzhou, in China, was managed via a central control system and saw the diminutive automatons get on down in perfect time. Some might find it a little spooky but at least when the robots take over, we can be sure they know how to party!

ROBOTIC WORLD'S BEST DANCERS

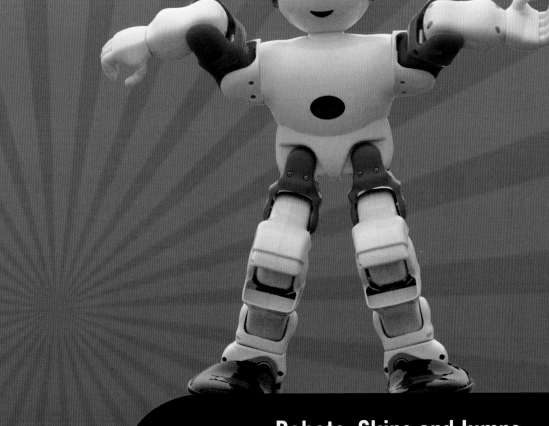

Robots, Skips and Jumps

http://y2u.be/9sUiLwxX4oM

Meet Jumpen, quite possibly the cutest robot ever – although that's not his official world record. Jumpen, a big-eyed blue-and-white robot penguin, was built at the National Institute of Technology Nara College, in Chiba, Japan. He was the outstanding winner of a skipping competition at a robot convention in Tokyo. For each skip to count, the rope had to complete a 360-degree revolution and be cleared by Jumpen. By the time 60 seconds had elapsed, the diminutive electronic being had completed a world-record 106 skips, successfully clearing the rope every single time. Altogether now, awwww!

ULTIMATE SKIPPING ROBOT PENGUIN

SEEING IS BELIEVING

How often do you hear or read of a record and think, "Surely that's just not possible." If only you could see for yourself …

GLASS- AND RECORD- BREAKING SINGER

Miniature Machine

http://y2u.be/cSg-yFZ7y0A

In the UK it's called a Heath Robinson contraption, while in the US they call it a Rube Goldberg machine. In France it's an *usine à gaz* (gas refinery), but the Germans come closest to describing it, calling it a *Was-passiert-dann-Maschine* (what-happens-next machine). This video features the smallest ever of these complex devices. Made with incredible precision for an advert for Japanese watch company Seiko, this intricate and beautiful machine uses 1,200 mechanical watch parts, some of which are smaller than a millimetre in size. In action, it's mesmerizing and rather magical.

◀ Vocal Re-chord

http://y2u.be/Ia57VfDaESw

Watch those glasses and windows if soul and R&B singer Georgia Brown is in town – and don't worry if the dog acts a little funny – for Georgia is renowned for one special vocal quality: she sings the highest note ever hit in the world. It's known as G10 and it's not actually a note but a frequency. Georgia's vocal cords effortlessly reach the so-called (and little understood) whistle register. This is the highest register of the human voice, way beyond soprano, falsetto and anything produced by a musical instrument.

▶ There's the Catch

http://y2u.be/7J4xw_g-WsA

Juggling. No! Don't skip this one straightaway. It's short and really impressive. Dutchman Niels Duinker is no children's party juggler; he's a multiple-record-holder and a serial champion in his field. Niels, whose show is entitled "Gravity is a Joke", has been juggling since the age of 12 and claims to have spent over 15,000 hours honing his craft. It seems to be time well spent too. In 2015 he set the bar for the cup-juggling world record at 12 cups. Then, in October 2017, he went two better. Awesome.

WORLD'S BEST CUP JUGGLER

▼ Flying Bum

http://y2u.be/CWiRZXW8t5I

Just why they call it the "Flying Bum" you can judge for yourself. The *Airlander 10*, part plane and part airship, is the world's largest aircraft. It's enormous: 302 feet (92 metres) long – about 50 feet/15 metres longer than the biggest passenger jets – with a cargo capacity of 10 metric tons. The aircraft is eco-friendly, silent, capable of a speed of 90 mph (148 km/h), and is able to land on practically any terrain. It can remain airborne for up to five days on manned flights, but can also float, unmanned, for weeks at a time.

On the Ball

http://y2u.be/GXsacavxteM

There doesn't have to be a point! That's the mantra of Great Ball Contraption (GBC) enthusiasts. A GBC is a machine that receives balls from one module and passes them to another module, rather like a bucket brigade (or the final contraption in the game Mousetrap). In a hotly contested competition, Maico Arts and Ben Jonkman won back their record for the world's largest Lego GBC with a madcap system of a hundred inter-connected lifts, slides and chutes. To give you an idea of quite how complex the contraption course is, it takes the ball 16 minutes and 30 seconds to travel from start to finish.

137

COOL CAR STUNTS

Car stunts are some of the most exciting clips on the site. These drivers risk life and limb to perform incredible record-breaking tricks and skills on four wheels.

▶ Wheelie Something

http://y2u.be/ggVpCOT9ZqY

Pulling a side-wheelie (driving on just one front and back wheel) in a car is a technically difficult and ludicrously dangerous feat. To drive along on two wheels at breakneck speed is taking it to another level. The speed record on two wheels was last set in 1997, so hats off to Finnish stunt driver Vesa Kivimäki, who finally broke the record in October 2016. Driving a BMW 330 fitted with tyres specially developed by sponsor Nokian, Kivimäki clocked 115.74 mph (186.269 km/h) in his record-breaking jaunt along the runway at Seinajoki Airport in the southwest of Finland.

▶ A Hard Truck Story

http://y2u.be/9Jw-TqA4U6I

Why did the 4x4 truck climb the obstacle? To get to the other side, of course! But this was no ordinary truck and no normal obstacle. The truck was a Czech-manufactured Tatra 810, and the obstacle, the Brutt Monster, was the world's highest artificially created obstacle – an extreme steel barrier arcing to 24.6 feet (7.5 metres) high, with a 55-degree incline. It was down to driver Libor Václavík to take on the Monster, a tricky task requiring him to assess the potential of the vehicle, his own driving skills and the laws of physics.

CAR VERSUS WORLD'S BIGGEST OBSTACLE

138

Tyred Out

http://y2u.be/38hlxUuzx2oJ

The Aussies love a burnout – where the brakes keep a vehicle stationary while spinning its wheels, causing the tyres to heat up and smoke due to friction. Burnout competitions thrive in Australia, where drivers use modified cars with no rear brakes. At the Summernats car festival in Canberra, billed as Australia's biggest horsepower party, 69 cars took part in the world-record attempt for a simultaneous 30-second burnout. Dozens of rather pricey tyres were shredded and some even ignited into small rubber fires as the entire area filled up with clouds of smoke.

▼ Practice Makes Perfect

http://y2u.be/febbQ4dvjUk

This looks so good. Fabulously shot with in-truck and under-truck cameras and the fantastic setting of a New Mexican ghost town, you almost don't care about the record. Bryce Menzies launches his two-wheel drive truck over the ramp and covers 379.2 feet (115.6 metres), beating the previous record by nearly 50 feet (15 metres). But that isn't the whole story. This jump was only a practice but, just after completing it, he wrote off the truck, fracturing his shoulder in the process. He was supposed to perform the feat on live TV but couldn't. Fortunately it didn't matter because this glorious footage was in the can.

THE LONG-
DISTANCE RAMP
JUMP RECORD

SMASHING
THE JUMP
RECORD

▼ Ramping It Up

http://y2u.be/L5N7R9Wbe_E

This is the closest you will ever come to seeing a flying car. It was New Year's Eve in Long Beach, California, in 2009, and 20,000 people had come out to see all-action driver Travis Pastrana try something really crazy. Pastrana, a rally champion turned stunt driver, launched his Subaru Impreza STI rally car off a ramp on the Pine Avenue Pier at 91 mph (146.6 km/h). He soared over Rainbow Harbor before successfully landing on a floating barge 269 feet (82 metres) away – almost 100 feet (30 metres) more than the former jump record.

PET RECORDS

These cool creatures have been officially verified as the biggest, sportiest, smallest and most agile.

▶ Monster Bunny

http://y2u.be/SbADYnhHtGg

Darius the rabbit weighs in at three-and-a-half stone (22.2 kilograms) and is the size of a small child. He's the biggest rabbit in the world, but Darius is no freak. His breed, the giant continental, produces large creatures and his mother Alice held the record before him. Five-year-old Darius stretches out to an amazing 4 feet, 4 inches (1.32 metres) long and munches through 4,000 carrots, 120 cabbages and 730 dog bowls of rabbit mix over the year.

THE WORLD'S BIGGEST RABBIT

Who's a Clever Girl Then?

http://y2u.be/unO5whIUF-M

YouTube is full of videos of dogs, and sometimes cats, performing stunts – but Kili the Senegal parrot can match them trick for trick. She claims an unofficial world record by pulling off 20 tricks in just under two minutes. Her feats begin with the customary parrot skills such as rope climbing and nodding. Nothing remarkable there, but carry on watching and you'll see Kili go bowling, match rings to pegs and perform a basketball slam dunk. Worthy of the record books, surely?

◢ Bunny Hoops

http://y2u.be/PWDSKplf9UU

Have you ever seen *Space Jam*, the 1996 movie starring basketball legend Michael Jordan alongside Bugs Bunny, Daffy Duck and other cartoon heroes? No? Well, never mind, watch this instead – the real-life version. Meet Bini the basketball-playing bunny. Apparently, he practices every night, and his commitment and training has paid off. This clip features Bini's world-record attempt for the most slam dunks by a rabbit in one minute – a prize as coveted in the animal realm as it is in the cartoon world.

BEST BASKET-BALLING BUNNY

Dog's Chance

http://y2u.be/68PMF7Xxppl

Alex Rothacker, a professional dog handler from Illinois, USA, takes in dogs that are often on the verge of being put down due to their aggression. Sweet Pea, an Australian shepherd/border collie mix, was one such dog who thrived under Alex's regime. Sweet Pea holds a rather strange record – the most steps walked down backwards by a dog while balancing a 5-ounce (140-gram) glass of water on its head. She achieved 10 and here she even does it blindfolded! Sweet Pea became a celebrity in Germany after appearing on a prime-time TV show, but died a few years ago at the age of 19.

▶ My Little Pony

http://y2u.be/6XQtd9cTGFM

Here's another Einstein. Smaller than most human babies he was just 14 inches (35.5 centimetres) high at birth, weighing only 6 pounds (2.7 kilograms). Now fully grown, Einstein stands 20 inches (50.8 centimetres) high and is officially the World's Smallest Stallion. The smallest horse, Thumbalina, is slightly shorter but, unlike her, Einstein is not a dwarf, he is just a mini miniature horse. He does, however, have a big personality. He has his own Facebook page, has appeared on *Oprah* and even had a book written about him.

THE WORLD'S SMALLEST STALLION

APP APTITUDE

It's the digital age and a new breed of record-breakers – tweeters, texters, vloggers and bloggers – is on the rise. These guys are setting amazing new standards – a bit more impressive than managing to remember your eight-digit password.

Avatar Assembly

http://y2u.be/HPUjg-6nufw

Fans of *World of Warcraft* – the most popular multi-player online role-playing game in the world – were briefly distracted from pursuing quests and fighting monsters to witness a record-breaking diorama. To promote a new expansion of their game at a convention, producers Blizzard created a 1,300-square-foot (400-square-metre) 3D battle, complete with over 10,000 3D printed figures. And just to make the world's largest video-game diorama completely fabulous, every character on the battlefield corresponded to convention attendees' avatars, including their armour, race and weaponry. Great! Now back to the game…

◀ Reality Check

http://y2u.be/yLGMEt3RkAg

There are worse places to spend 36 hours – the dentist, a motorway service station or your aunt's wedding, perhaps? Jack McNee from Sydney, Australia, did his record time in the virtual world. There are many pastimes available on VR, including colonizing alien planets or exploring the ocean, but Jack played *Tilt Brush* for the whole time! With the device strapped to his face for a day and a half, he painted and played *Hangman* and *Pictionary* with his YouTube live-stream viewers. As for eating and comfort breaks, Jack relied on his trusty staff to guide him.

LONGEST TIME SPENT IN VIRTUAL REALITY

▼ Fastest Finger

http://y2u.be/zXjTPnV8ZvM

Fancy a go at being the fastest texter in the world? Here's your chance. Get your phone or iPad set up and see how fast you can type (or swype) the following sentence: "The razor-toothed piranhas of the genera Serrasalmus and Pygocentrus are the most ferocious freshwater fish in the world. In reality they seldom attack a human." Did you make it under 17.5 seconds? If you did, get your claim off to the record-keepers. If not, watch this clip of record-holder Abdul Basit showing just how it's done.

THE FASTEST TEXTER OF ALL TIME

A Man Needs His Nuggs

http://y2u.be/4k1JzcES0G0

In April 2017, 16-year-old Carter Wilkerson tweeted the fast-food restaurant Wendy's asking how many retweets it would take to get a year of free chicken nuggets. The food chain's considered reply? 18 million. Considering that Ellen's famous Oscar selfie generated 3.42 million (the most retweeted of all time), it was a big ask but, when Carter retweeted the message to his 170 followers, saying "HELP ME PLEASE. A MAN NEEDS HIS NUGGS", the response was incredible. The quest captured the public's imagination and Carter sailed past the record. He was still way short of the required total but, nonetheless, Wendy's decently provided the year's supply of nuggets.

SPORTS HEROES

From the sublime skills of Cristiano Ronaldo to the stars of quirky sports such as bog snorkelling or walking on your hands, these people are all record heroes.

MULTIPLE FOOTBALL-RECORD HOLDER

Round the Twist

http://y2u.be/oLgQLZIA0hM

The world is a small place when it comes to record-breaking. In every continent, in some backyard, park or community space there is someone trying to break a record. Here we are in far-flung Kathmandu, in Nepal, where Dinesh "Parkour" Sunar, a local police officer and sometime Bollywood stuntman, attempts a record for twisting back-flips off a wall. Each flip must contain a mid-air 360-degree rotation backwards and a 360-degree barrel-roll twist, with the jumper landing facing the wall. No problem for Dinesh. He racks up a mighty 18 in the allotted minute.

▼ CR7 Heaven

http://y2u.be/JJeHBnJZE_0

Love him or hate him, there is no denying the heights that footballer Cristiano Ronaldo has reached. The man they call CR7 has so many domestic and international football records, including scoring in every minute of a game, scoring the most Champions League goals, and being the only player to win every major trophy with two different clubs. In 2017 his three goals against the Faroe Islands saw him pass Pele's record of four international hat-tricks and, by the end of the year, he was just seven goals short of the international goal-scoring record. Will this be his next feat? Don't bet against it.

▼ Seconds Out

http://y2u.be/BSp60Y-eLR0

Zolani Tete versus Siboniso Gonya wasn't top of the bill at Belfast in November 2017. The next morning, however, it was the bout people were talking about, even though it lasted just 11 seconds and consisted of a single punch. WBO bantamweight champion Tete was expected to win – just not like this. The 29-year-old South African laid out his countryman, landing a brutal right hook six seconds after the opening bell. The referee officially ended the contest five seconds later as the challenger lay sprawled out. It was the quickest-ever world-title fight in the history of boxing.

▼ Muddy the Waters

http://y2u.be/UoRXZOQBsSQ

The World Bog Snorkelling Championship, first held in 1985, takes place every August at the dense Waen Rhydd peat bog, near Llanwrtyd Wells in Mid-Wales. Bog snorkelling requires competitors to complete two consecutive 60-yard (55-metre) lengths of a water-filled trench cut through a peat bog. Competitors must wear snorkels and flippers, and complete the course without using conventional swimming strokes, relying on flipper power alone. Andrew Holmes is the record holder with a time of 84 seconds.

White Knuckle Walk

http://y2u.be/7i_xFbfptpg

What happens in your lunchtime at school or in the office? I bet it's not as exciting as watching Slava Popov walk around the canteen upside-down, as he does in this clip. The Russian – a former acrobat, and coach to Cirque du Soleil performers – runs a company called Handstand Body Control that teaches fitness through handstand techniques. The fully in-control Slava is a pretty good advert for his company. Watch from two minutes in as he breaks the record for walking on his fists. He covers 108 feet (33 metres) with ease and looks like he could continue down the high street and back.

THE WORLD BOG SNORKELLING CHAMPION

▼ Cheese Chase

http://y2u.be/xHE3wsQ7Wy0

The Coopers Hill annual event is the oldest cheese-rolling competition in the world. A 9-pound (4-kilogram) Double Gloucester cheese is chased down the hill. The first person to catch it is the winner. However, since the cheese has a one-second start and reaches speeds of 70 mph (113 km/h), this is usually just a race for the finish. Stephen Gyde is the most successful competitor ever with 21 cheeses, and the only competitor to have won all three cheeses in a single year.

CHEESE-ROLLING RECORDS

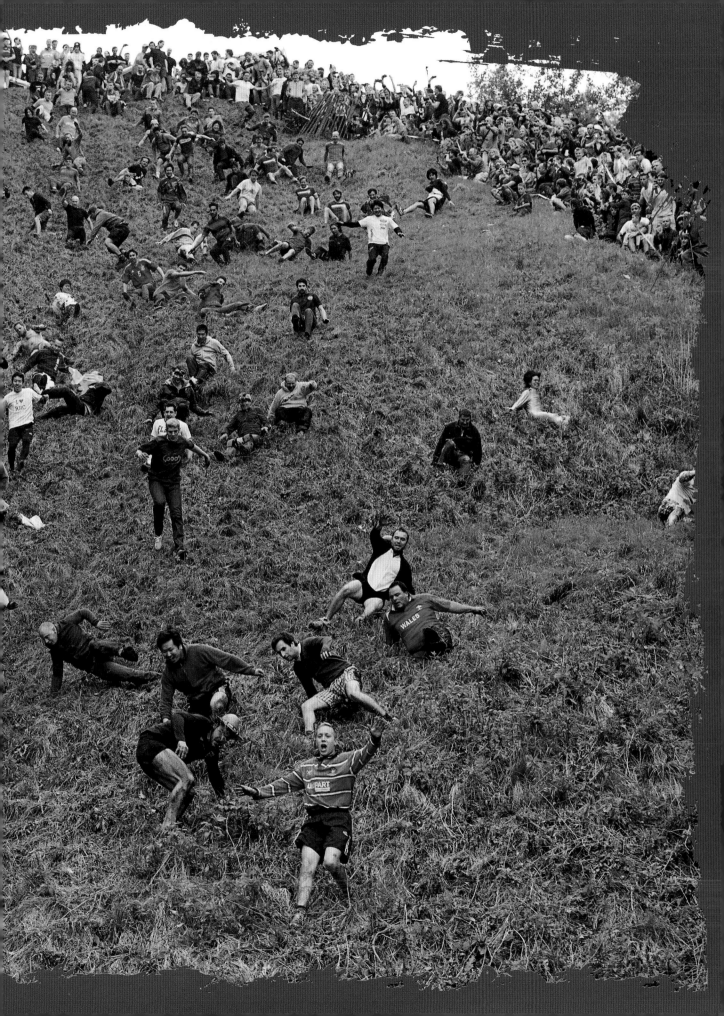

COOL SPORTS RECORDS

From frantic four-legged running to bionic shoes, the quest for sporting perfection never ends and with it comes the sound of clattering records.

Spiderman

http://y2u.be/vP5Gn6BdTQg

Ready for some real-life Spiderman action? Sport climbing is due to be an Olympic sport in Tokyo 2020 and it should be a real crowd-pleaser. Here's a taster – the 15-metre speed-climbing world record. Czech speed climber Libor Hroza is a star of the sport and shins up the wall in astonishing fashion, skimming 0.12 seconds off his record. Wall climbing is a lightning-fast event so don't blink or you'll miss it. In fact, it's done in a little over five seconds. As one wag says in the comments, "I can't even get out of bed in five seconds!"

FOUR-LEGGED-SPRINT RECORD HOLDER

▶ Four Legs Good

http://y2u.be/A3rcWarJOe0

Kenici Ito, a 29-year-old man from Tokyo, Japan, spent over eight years perfecting a four-legged running style based on the wiry Patas monkey of Africa. Neighbours would see him walking around on all fours and he was even shot at by mistake by hunters when training in the mountains. It all paid off in 2012, when Ito incredibly ran 100 metres in less than 20 seconds. He now runs in four-legged races but admits he is still beaten by a fast dog.

Bionic Boot

http://y2u.be/1jvKaM7R5iY

The ostrich is an unlikely inspiration for a shoe. However, San Francisco-based inventor Keahi Seymour looked at a bird that can reach speeds of 40 mph (70 km/h) and covers up to 16 feet (5 metres) in a single stride, and created a boot to imitate the ostrich's action. His shoes have springs on the back and enable runners to reach 25 mph (40 km/h), slightly short of Usain Bolt's 27.44 mph (44 km/h), but they can keep going for longer than 328 feet (100 metres) – and Seymour assures us they are only going to get faster.

▲ Going Gaga

http://y2u.be/txXwg712zw4

Lady Gaga has claimed a host of Guinness World Records throughout her glittering career, but she really stole the show at the 2017 Super Bowl. First, she appeared to leap from the roof of the stadium onto the stage in front of her hordes of adoring fans. The pop star then went on to perform the most-watched live musical show in history, with over 150 million people watching her dance her way through her biggest hits during the half-time show. The crowd seemed pretty disappointed when she had to leave the stage so that the NFL match could resume...

Pedal Power

http://y2u.be/CkQGATSscs4

Ever wondered why cyclists choose to ride just inches from the bike in front? It's not to get a good look at their backside, but to take advantage of "drafting". Tucked in a vortex, sheltered from the wind, they are "carried" along by the air pocket and save between 20 and 40 per cent of energy expenditure. So that's why Brazilian former pro-cyclist Evandro Portela rides behind an SUV, modified with a rear canopy, when performing his record attempt. It was worth it. Evandro went where no cyclist had been before – to a speed of 125.5 mph (202 km/h)!

WHAT A RECORD!

If God had meant us to fly, he'd have given us wings ... then again, he did give us skateboards, huge swings, dodgy planes and long bungee elastic!

The Only Way is Down

http://y2u.be/JXyQ3N4S5oc

Marc Sluszny is the most extreme adventurer in the world. He's set a world record in bungee jumping, dived with a great white shark and represented Belgium in tennis, fencing, yachting and bobsleigh. In 2012, Marc found a new hobby – running down a building. Here he is completing a vertical run down the side of the Belgacom tower in Brussels. The tower is 335 feet (102 metres) high and he sprinted down the outside of it in a time of 15.5 seconds – a new world record.

▼ Hairpin Highway Dash

http://y2u.be/j7hrJzjKEys

Tongtian Road's nickname is "Heaven-Linking Avenue". It takes visitors to the "Gateway to Heaven" – a natural cave on the side of the Tianmen Mountain in China – but the name also hints at the perils of one of the world's most dangerous roads. Twisting alongside sheer drops, the 6.8-mile (11-kilometre) road zig-zags through 99 sharp turns, rising from 656 feet (200 metres) to 4,265 feet (1,300 metres) above sea level. In a specially modified Ferrari, racing driver Fabio Barone Mihaela set a record when he sped along the treacherous route in just 10 minutes and 31 seconds.

▶ The "1080"

http://y2u.be/tbjzZHuGTng

In March 2012, at the age of 12, Tom Schaar became a skateboarding legend. Less than a year after becoming the youngest skateboarder (and only the eighth ever) to successfully land a "900" (2.5 revolutions in the air), he landed a three-revolution "1080". He was the first skateboarder to successfully attempt the feat despite many efforts from leading boarders. Tom, who expected to spend all day trying to complete the move, nailed it on only his fifth attempt.

THE WORLD'S FIRST "1080"

▲ Big Rush

http://y2u.be/FrY6OJk-z0I

The Moses Mabhida Stadium in Durban, South Africa, was built for the FIFA World Cup in 2010. The imposing 54,000-seater venue, instantly recognizable from its beautiful white arches, now hosts sports matches, events and the world's only stadium swing – the biggest swing of any kind. Those venturing to the top of the stadium are afforded a fabulous 360-degree view of Durban and a chance to ride the Big Rush Adrenaline Swing. This thrilling experience begins with a 288-foot (88-metre) freefall followed by a massive 721-foot (220-metre) arc that takes the rider into the centre of the stadium. Not for the faint-hearted!

WORLD'S BIGGEST SWING

▲ Flight of Fancy

http://y2u.be/KUIZQ3JyrBM

Man cracked the secret of flying more than a hundred years ago, but you wouldn't think it watching the Red Bull Flugtag. Held annually since 1992 all around the world, the "flying day" event sees participants build and then pilot their homemade flying machines off a 28-foot (8.5-metre) high flight deck. Judged for distance, creativity and showmanship, the aerodynamic qualities of the aircraft are often questionable. Many teams crash pretty instantly and chaotically into the waters below. However, in 2013 the Chicken Whisperers team set a distance record of 258 feet (78.64 metres) in Long Beach, California.

In Full Swing

http://y2u.be/xkqTDtYPuho

Think back to those carefree days in the playground and getting some real height on the swings. Didn't you always wonder whether you could go over the top and complete a 360-degree swing? Welcome to the sport of Kiiking. Invented in 1996 in Estonia, Kiiking sees adults swinging on massive swings with telescopic steel arms that can be extended for each competitor. Although now practised around the world, the record is fittingly held by an Estonian, former Olympic rower Kaspar Taimsoo. Now, you don't see that kind of thing down the park…

WORLD'S MOST CREATIVE AIRCRAFT

HAIR-RAISING RECORDS

There are some special people for whom "doing their hair" doesn't mean a few minutes with a brush and a mirror. Hairstyles, beards, moustaches and other follicular follies are their step to stardom ...

▶ High and Mighty

http://y2u.be/vl3imFyfBU8

You'll know the hi-top fade when you see it. The afro-style haircut – short on the back and sides but big on top – was popular in the 1990s. It was, perhaps, most famously worn by Will Smith in the early seasons of *The Fresh Prince of Bel-Air* and is now enjoying a revival. That won't be harmed by US model Benny Harlem, who broke the Internet in 2016 with pictures of his and his daughter's beautiful and natural hair, and then, a year later, produced a 20.5-inch (52-centimetre) high hairstyle, which broke a world record for tallest hi-top fade.

THE WORLD'S TALLEST HI-TOP

◀ Blow-Dry Bunny

http://y2u.be/iUZgEFRoIX8

English Angora rabbits are the supermodels of the rabbit world, regularly sweeping up the prizes at shows. Looking like a basketball-sized cotton-wool ball, they're incredibly cute and the only rabbit that has hair covering its eyes. Prize-winning Angora breeder Betty Chu has 50 of them, and not only does she take them to competitions, but she uses their wool to knit hats, scarves and mittens. The most famous of them is Francesca, whose sumptuous fur won her the accolade of the rabbit with the longest hair in the world – her coat measured in at 14.37 inches (36.5 centimetres).

THE WORLD'S LONGEST MOHICAN

▼ Hard to Handlebar

http://y2u.be/PKzBzDY5I50

Ram Singh Chauhan of India is the proud owner of the world's longest moustache, stretching an incredible 14 feet (4.27 metres). Now 57, he started growing his moustache in 1970. It isn't an easy life – Chauhan spends an hour every day cleaning and combing his moustache, and when it is not on proud display, he has to neatly wrap it around his neck. However, it has brought him prestige and some fame, with appearances in Bollywood films as well as the 1983 James Bond film *Octopussy*.

▲ The Vast of the Mohicans

http://y2u.be/X__XlPhgH34

Usually, Kazuhiro Watanabe's hair is clipped up so it doesn't drag around his knees. It has taken the Japanese fashion designer 15 years to grow it that long, but it is all part of his record-breaking plan. When Kazuhiro gets dressed up (usually for an outdoor event), he and his stylists go to work with three cans of hair spray and an entire bottle of hair gel. Just three hours later, he has the world's highest Mohican – a spike that is a massive 3 feet, 8.6 inches (1.13 metres) high.

THE LONGEST MOUSTACHE IN THE WORLD

SETTING YOUR OWN RECORD

Even in our wildest dreams, we can't hope to emulate the feats of some of the record breakers in this book. The achievements of Usain Bolt or Cristiano Ronaldo are the result of a talent and dedication possessed by few. Others are born to be record breakers by dint of an exceptional physical attribute – a long tongue, big feet – whether they like it or not! Still, the budding record breaker need not despair. There are plenty of videos in this book to inspire anyone to write their name in the history books.

Perhaps you already have a unique skill or hobby that can rival the record holders. For example, you might have a great talent for skipping or licking your nose or you might have quick reflexes or a steady hand. It is likely that your particular skill isn't yet at the level of the current record holders; most of the achievements in the book are due to practice and hard graft. Start working at it now, though, and who knows what heights you will reach?

You don't have to possess a great physical skill to enter the record books. There are plenty of other entries that are equally impressive. Mental agility is a popular area and there are incredible feats of reading, mathematics and memory; world-beating collections – of anything from TV-show memorabilia to cereal packets – form a fascinating aspect of record breaking; and someone needs to organize the large-scale gatherings that beat records.

If you need to research your goal, go online and check the existing record. Some in this book did just that and discovered it was a target they could aspire to and eventually beat. There are various organizations, including sporting bodies, who keep their own statistics. Most famously, the *Guinness Book of Records* (www. guinnessworldrecords.com) has been keeping records since 1955 and has a comprehensive database and an online application process.

If you are looking to set a more unusual record, it might be worth consulting recordsetter.com, where you will find inspiration and challenges for all kinds of records – many of which can be attempted in your own kitchen or bedroom. If you don't fancy taking on other people's records, you can always invent your own category. You'll definitely have a record, but don't count on keeping it for long – it's a mighty competitive record-breaking world.

INDEX

159

PICTURE CREDITS

The publishers would like to thank the following sources for their kind permission to reproduce the pictures in this book.

Page 4 AFP Photo/Vano Shlamov/Getty Images, 5 Peter Parks/AFP/Getty Images, 7 Arkaprava Ghosh/Barcroft India, 8 (left) Paulo Whitaker/Reuters, (right) Jarno Cordia/courtesy of Harvard PR, 9 Fotodive.ch/Wilfried Niedermayr, 10 (left) Arkaprava Ghosh/Barcroft India, (right) Courtesy of William Winram, 11 Marc de Boer/Alamy, 12 (top) Thomas Deco/Shutterstock, (bottom) Kathy Hutchins/Shutterstock, 13 M4OS Photos/Alamy, 14 (top) Katerina Graghine/Shutterstock, (bottom) Claudia Naerdemann/Shutterstock, 15 (top) Hagen Hopkins/Getty Images, (bottom) Chris24/Alamy, 16 (left) Jia Li/Shutterstock, (right) Shaun Botterill/Getty Images, 17 (top) Halldor Bjornsson/Alamy, (bottom) Cameron Spencer/Getty Images, 18 Stan Honda/AFP/Getty Images, 19 (top) Shutterstock, (bottom) Universal History Archive/UIG via Getty Images, 20 (top) Shutterstock, (bottom) Mark Moffett/Minden Pictures/Getty Images, 21-23 Shutterstock, 24 Bettmann/Getty, 25 (top) AFP Photo/Vano Shlamov/Getty Images (bottom) Drew Simon/AP/Press Association Images, 26 Ken McKay/ITV/REX/Shutterstock, 27 Shutterstock, 28 muzsy/Shutterstock, 29 (top) Julian Finney/Getty Images, (bottom) Shutterstock, 30 (left) Gregory Varnum/Wikimedia Commons, (right) PitK/Shutterstock, 31 TowersStreet, 32-33 Shutterstock, 34 Fred Duval/FilmMagic/Getty Images, 35 Shutterstock, 36 (left) Nils Jorgensen/REX/Shutterstock, (right) Erin Hull/The Washington Post/Getty Images, 37 (top) Drozdowski/Shutterstock, (bottom) Shutterstock, 38 Getty Images, 39. Mario Tama/Getty Images, 40 (top) Shutterstock, (bottom) ZUMA Press, Inc/Alamy, 41 (top) Matt Cardy/Getty images, (bottom) Jagadeesh NV.EPE-EFE/REX/Shutterstock, 42-43 Shutterstock, 44 Mark Rolston/AFP/Getty Images, 45 (top) Thomas Senf/Red Bull News Ro/Sipa/REX/Shutterstock, (bottom) Photo by Rauke Schalken with Leica, 46-47 WENN Ltd/Alamy, 48 (left) Shutterstock, (right) Moviestore Collection/REX/Shutterstock, 49 (top) Angus Murray/Sports Illustrated/Getty Images, (bottom) Ethan Miller/Getty Images, 50-51 Ray Tang/REX/Shutterstock, 52-53 USN Collection/Alamy, 54 (top) Shutterstock, (bottom) John Robertson/Barcroft Media/Getty Images, 55 (top) Angela Weiss/Getty Images, (bottom) Shutterstock, 56 Shutterstock, 57 (top) Shutterstock, (bottom) mb123/Shutterstock, 58 dpa/Alamy, 59 (top) DFree/Shutterstock (bottom) Ian MacNicol/Getty Images, 60 East News/REX/Shutterstock, 61 (top) Zhukov Oleg/Shutterstock, (bottom) Evan Down Load/Shutterstock, 62-63 Shutterstock, 64 (left) Artem Zamula/Shutterstock, 64-65 Gaizka Iroz/AFP/Getty Images, 65 (top) Evikka/Shutterstock, 66 Lee Young Ho/Sipa USA/REX/Shutterstock, 67 Kevin Mazur/WireImage/Getty Images, 68 Shutterstock, 69 (top) Shutterstock, (bottom) Getty Images, 70 Shutterstock, 71 (top) Gent Shkullaku/AFP/Getty Images, (bottom) Obuda University, 72 (top) Shutterstock, (bottom) Vitalina Rybakova/Shutterstock, 73 (top) Vano Shlamov/AFP/Getty Images, (bottom) Victor Fraile/Getty Images, 74 (top) Geoffrey Robinson/REX/Shutterstock (bottom) Prathan Nakdontree/Shutterstock, 75 Katherine Frey/The Washington Post/Getty Images, 76 Shutterstock, 77 (top) Shutterstock, (bottom) Yuriy Dyachyshyn/AFP/Getty Images, 78 Createthis/Shutterstock, 79 (top) Laurentiu Garofeanu/Barcoft Media/Getty Images, (bottom) Splash News, 80 Dave Mangels/Getty Images, 81 (top) The Siberian Times, (bottom) Press Trust of India, 82-83 Piti A Sahakorn/LightRocket/Getty Images, 84 (top) Josh Edelson/AFP/Getty Images, (bottom) Shutterstock, 85 (top) Matt Writtle/Barcroft Media/Getty Images, (bottom) Barry Bland/Barcroft Media/Getty Images, 86 Mr.Whiskey/Shutterstock, 87 (left) Phil Rees/Alamy, (right) Barcroft Media/Getty Images, 88 XiXinXing/Shutterstock, 89 (top) PA Images, (bottom) Stacie McChesney/NBC/NBCU Photo Bank/Getty Images, 90 (centre) Shutterstock, (bottom) Yamil Lage/AFP/Getty Images, 90-91 Francisco Leong/AFP/Getty Images, 92 Imaginechina, 93 (top) Lily Hevesh/Barcroft Media/Getty Images, (bottom left) Gonzales Photo/Demotix, (bottom right) Shutterstock, 94-95 Liam Cleary/Demotix, 96 Ilya S. Savenok/Getty Images, 97 Petri Oeschger/Gallo Images/Getty Images, 98-99 Imaginechina/REX/Shutterstock, 100 (left) AF archive/Alamy, (right) Kena Betancur/AFP/Getty Images, 101 (top) Egorov Artem/Shutterstock, (bottom) Matt Alexander/PA Images, 102 Simon Stacpoole/REX/Shutterstock, 103 (right) Laurence Griffiths/Getty Images, (bottom) Markus Scholz/DPA/PA Images, 104 Ruaridh Connellan/Barcroft USA/Getty Images, 105 (top) Inga Ivanova/Shutterstock, (bottom) Jack Ludlam/Alamy, 106 Shutterstock, 107 (top) Steve Russell/Toronto Star/Getty Images, (bottom) terstock, 108-109 Jim Watson/AFP/Getty Images, 110 FOX/Getty Images, 111 (top) Shutterstock (bottom), Ruaridh Connellan/Barcroft USA/Getty Images, 112 Shutterstock, 113 Kuttelvaserova Stuchelova/Shutterstock,

114-115 Mark Campbell/REX/Shutterstock, 116 (top) Etihad Airways/Getty Images, (bottom) Kirsty Wigglesworth/AP/REX/Shutterstock, 117 (top) Enrique De La Osa/Reuters, (bottom) Christophe Petit Tesson/EPA/REX/Shutterstock, 118 Shutterstock, 119 (top) Roy Dabner/EPA/REX/Shutterstock, (bottom) VCG/Getty Images, 120 (top) Eric Sakowski, (bottom) Wan Cheuk Nang/Shutterstock, 121 (top) Imaginechina/REX/Shutterstock, (centre) © Raymond Cunningham, (bottom) Shutterstock, 122 Shutterstock, 123 (top) Michael Potter11/Shutterstock, (bottom) RSPCA, 124 NASA, 125 (top) Visharo/Shutterstock, (bottom) Zhejiang University, 126 (left) Geraldo Caso/AFP/Getty Images, (right) Aflo/REX/Shutterstock, 127 Austral Int./REX/Shutterstock, 128 (top) Johan Ordonez/AFP/Getty Images, (bottom) Phillip Maguire/Shutterstock, 129 (top) HAP/Quirky China News/REX/Shutterstock, (bottom) Shutterstock, 130-131 Adnan Abidi/Reuters, 132 (top) Shutterstock, (bottom) Sipa Asia/REX/Shutterstock, 133 (top) Pau Barrena/AFP/Getty Images, (bottom) Jeff Spicer/Leapfrog Films/Getty Images, 134 Shutterstock, 135 Imaginechina/REX/Shutterstock, 136 Kameel4u/Shutterstock, 137 (top) Kai Keisuke/Shutterstock, (bottom) Justin Tallis/AFP/Getty Images, 138 (top) Nokian Tyres, (bottom) Sojka Libor/Czech News Agency/PA Images, 139 Cristiano Barni/Shutterstock, 140-141 Garth Milan/Red Bull Photofiles/Getty Images, 142 Caters News Agency, 143 (top) Warner Bros./Everett Collection/Alamy, (bottom) Katie Greene/Bellingham Herald/MCT/Getty Images, 144 (top) Blizzard Entertainment Inc. (bottom) UfaBizPhoto/Shutterstock, 145 (top) theskaman306/Shutterstock, (bottom) Jim Watson/AFP/Getty Images, 146 Marcos Mesa Sam Wordley/Shutterstock, 147 REX/Shutterstock, 148-149 Justin Tallis/AFP/Getty Images, 150 Toru Yamanaka/AFP/Getty Images, 151 Kevin Mazur/Wireimage/Getty Images, 152 (centre) Imaginechina/REX/Shutterstock, (bottom) Peter Parks/AFP/Getty Images, 153 (top) Big Swing, (bottom) Anton Gvozdikov/Shutterstock, 154 (top) Moviestore Collection/REX/Shutterstock, (bottom) Steve Shott/Getty Images, 155 (left) Adrees Latif/Reuters, (right) Arkaprava Ghosh/Barcroft India, 160 Ken McKay/ITV/REX/Shutterstock

Every effort has been made to acknowledge correctly and contact the source and/or copyright holder of each picture and Carlton Books Limited apologises for any unintentional errors or omissions, which will be corrected in future editions of this book.